WITHDRAWN

INCOME DISTRIBUTION
Analysis and Policies

INCOME DISTRIBUTION
Analysis and Policies

JAN TINBERGEN

Emeritus Professor
Erasmus University Rotterdam

1975

NORTH-HOLLAND PUBLISHING COMPANY – AMSTERDAM · OXFORD
AMERICAN ELSEVIER PUBLISHING COMPANY, INC. – NEW YORK

Library of Congress Catalog Card Number: 74 – 30921
North-Holland ISBN: 0 7204 3094 1
American Elsevier ISBN: 0 444 10832 7

Publishers:

NORTH-HOLLAND PUBLISHING COMPANY – AMSTERDAM
NORTH-HOLLAND PUBLISHING COMPANY, LTD. – OXFORD

Sole distributors for the U.S.A. and Canada:

AMERICAN ELSEVIER PUBLISHING COMPANY, INC.
52 VANDERBILT AVENUE
NEW YORK, N.Y. 10017

Printed in The Netherlands

Foreword

This book constitutes a synthesis of a number of studies undertaken in the last five years and published as articles or as chapters of collective books. Its publication has been undertaken at the initiative of my former colleagues and collaborators in the Erasmus University of Rotterdam. I owe them a heavy debt of gratitude, especially to Professors H.C. Bos and L.B.M. Mennes and to Dr. P.A. Cornelisse, for the valuable suggestions they made in order to improve the presentation. I am equally indebted to the publishers of the studies mentioned previously, who kindly permitted reproduction of part of them, and to North-Holland for their willingness to publish this book. A list of the articles or chapters and their publishers will be found overleaf.

In a number of discussions on the subject matter I profited from critical remarks by staff members of the Centre for Development Planning, Erasmus University, in particular those made by J. George Waardenburg. Many of the calculations were also made by staff members and student assistants, for which help I am thankful too. The many remaining imperfections are, of course, entirely mine. The unpleasant task of correcting my English idiom was gracefully carried out by Ms. Susan Farr Wassenaar to whom I express my sincere thanks.

Ms. Suze van Willigenburg, with her usual skill and energy, was kind enough to undertake the task of typing the manuscript.

Last but not least, the ethical aspects of income distribution were the subject of many discussions with my wife Tine, whose care for myself and my work has protected me ever since we met.

Jan Tinbergen

This book draws heavily upon the following articles or chapters, all by the present author and published or to be published elsewhere.

'Trends in income distribution in some Western countries', in *International Trade and Money* by M.B. Conolly and A.K. Swoboda, eds. (George Allen and Unwin Ltd., London, 1973).

'Can income inequality be reduced further?', in *Festschrift für Walter Georg Waffenschmidt, zur Vollendung des 85. Lebensjahres* (Anton Hain Verlag, Meisenheim am Glan, 1972).

'The impact of education on income distribution', Review of Income and Wealth, Ser. 18, No. 3 (1972).

'Income inequality: Past, present, outlook', in *Urban and Social Economics in Market and Planned Economies: Vol. 2, Housing, income and environment* by Alan A. Brown, Joseph A. Licari and Egon Neuberger, eds. (Praeger Publishers, Inc., New York, 1974).

'Actual, feasible and optimal income inequality in a three-level education model', The Annals of the American Academy of Political and Social Science, Vol. 409 (1973).

'Substitution between types of labour in production', Giornale degli Economisti e Annali di Economia, No. 11/12 (1973).

'An interdisciplinary approach to the measurement of utility or welfare', Fifth Geary Lecture (The Economic and Social Research Institute, Dublin, 1972).

'Labour with different types of skills and jobs as production factors', De Economist, Vol. 121 (1973).

'Een raming van de Nederlandse inkomensverdeling omstreeks 1990', in *Liber Amicorum Prof. Dr. G. Eyskens*, forthcoming (1975).

'Substitution of graduate by other labour', Kyklos, Vol. 27, Fasc. 2 (1974).

'Equitable income distribution: Another experiment', to be published in a volume in honor of Professor Nicolas Georgescu-Roegen (1975).

'Technische Entwicklung und Einkommensverteilung', Zeitschrift für Wirtschaft- und Sozialwissenschaften', Vol. 1 (1974).

'Actual versus optimal income distribution in a three-level education model', in *Scritti in honore di Guglielmo Tagliacarne* (Roma, 1974).

'The demand–supply theory of income distribution', Frank W. Paish Lecture (1974).

'Personal characteristics and income', Lancaster Conference of the Royal Economic Society (1974).

Contents

1

Introduction

1.1. Main subjects of this book

The subjects dealt with in this book may be summarized as the analysis of figures on income distribution published by other authors – persons or institutions. The analysis revolves around three questions, namely:
(1) How can income inequality in developed countries be explained?
(2) How can it be reduced?
(3) What aims should be pursued in reducing it?

The way these questions are dealt with can be understood from the table of contents of the book.

The subjects to be dealt with can also be defined, in a negative way, by an enumeration of what the reader will not find in this book. The following subjects have been excluded:
(a) a critical discussion of what corrections have been applied by the authors quoted to the base material on incomes they used;
(b) the broad question of the optimal social order of which an optimal income distribution can be seen as a component;
(c) income distribution of developing countries, a subject on which especially Irma Adelman and Cynthia Taft Morris have pioneered.

This exclusion does not mean that connexions with these subjects have been entirely neglected. Still less does it mean that subjects (a)–(c) are considered of less importance; for each, the contrary is true. They have been excluded because a reasonably clear delimitation of this book's subject would seem possible along the frontiers described.

Exclusion of (b) also implies that hardly any attention has been given to the role played by capital income or capital gains. These subjects have been excluded mainly because many other authors have been dealing with them in considerable detail.

The structure of the present publication has been chosen as follows. In the remainder of this chapter a *bird's-eye view* is presented of the area covered as well as some of the adjacent territories. Chapter 2 summarizes some important *descriptions* of income inequality and its variation over time and among geographical areas. Chapter 3 sets out the main instrument of analysis used; it is the instrument of *supply and demand* analysis. The same chapter illustrates this instrument by estimations, from empirical material, of the so-called *price equation* for productive services, mainly labour. Since distribution is our subject, it is the distribution of these prices and hence of its determinants which is eventually dealt with. Chapter 4 deals with the supply side and its ultimate determinants, appearing in the *utility function* of the individuals or groups supplying labour of various kinds. Among determinants, *needs* and *capabilities available* play important roles. Chapter 5 considers the demand side and its ultimate source, *production functions*, expressed in terms of the various types of labour and hence of *capabilities required*. As a matter of course, questions of *substitution* between various types of labour and between capital and labour enter the picture. In addition, *technological development* will be introduced. Chapter 6 concentrates on what emerges as a central theme in the explanation of changing income inequalities: the *race* between *education* and *technological development*. While the preceding chapters contain some clues to the explanation of income inequality and some ways to influence it, Chapter 7 attempts to make a contribution to the *possible choice* of *aims*. In a simple complete econometric model for the Netherlands the numbers of individuals with first, second and third-level education are considered to be controllable within limits and the minimum possible (or *feasible*) inequality is estimated. In addition an optimality concept is proposed and *optimal* income inequality deduced. In Chapter 8 a definition of *equity* is proposed and used as an alternative aim. Chapter 9 discusses what *means* can be used to change income inequality and what the likely extent of their influence is. A comparison between *Western* and *Eastern* European countries illustrates the impact of the social order. Finally, Chapter 10 summarizes our findings.

1.2. Problems dealt with by various groups of authors

In the last decade or so numerous publications have dealt with the problem (i) of the determinants of income or of income distribution, as well as with the problems (ii) how, and (iii) to what extent, income distribution can be influenced. Already the three problems mentioned are different and should be clearly distinguished. Assuming that the determinants of income, defined in some way, have been found and their quantitative impact measured, income distribution can be derived from this result by taking some measure of income distribution, say its standard deviation, and correspondingly taking the standard deviations of all the determinants included in the equation 'explaining' income. Whether or not these results can be used to answer the question how income distribution can be influenced largely depends on the nature of the determinants chosen: if among them there are instruments of socio-economic policy, the answer can be given.

In all this a distinction should be made, moreover, between *direct* and *indirect* determinants. Most of the authors I am going to deal with have opted for the former alternative; in principle, however, a complete socio-economic model should be used, in which each relationship only describes direct determinants of one of the endogenous variables of the model. Income (or its distribution) can then be expressed in terms of the exogenous variables by eliminating all other endogenous variables. This yields the reduced form of the income variable equation and among the exogenous variables there will be, as a rule, a number of instruments.

Depending on the approach chosen three groups of scholars can be distinguished who recently have dealt with the problem of 'explaining' incomes. The first group consists of the well-known *human capital school* (the Schultzes [58, 59], Mincer [44, 45], Chiswick [14, 15, 16], Husén [31] and De Wolff and Van Slijpe [20], cf. Chapter 4). These authors concentrate their attention on the supply side of the market for production factors, mainly labour of various types. Demand is introduced only by including unemployment, typically a short-run treatment. On the supply side the capabilities available are the variables connecting price, that is income, with the quantities supplied. Only a few capabilities are available from statistical measurement and considerable gaps in our information on non-cognitive capabilities still have to be closed. Yet years of schooling and years of work experience together are able to explain a considerable portion of the variance of observations. I come back to both questions, especially in Chapter 4.

The second group may be called the *education planning school* and is represented by such authors as Bowles [5], Dougherty [21, 22] and Psacharopoulos [52]. They concentrate their attention on the demand side, deriving demand for various types of labour from production functions containing these types (cf. Chapter 5). So far they have alternatively described labour with the aid of capabilities, mainly schooling, and with the aid of the profession or job taken. I submit that categories of labour might be described by two suffixes, one for the quality offered and one for the quality required.

A third group of authors on the subject may be called the *demand and supply school*, since essentially they introduce both these sides of the market. One outstanding example is Freeman [24] and another Ullman [74]. I adhere to this group and made some attempts to combine the excellent work of all three groups (cf. Chapters 3 and 6). As an alternative to production functions I also used dummies for the demand side; a very simple one is the average income level of the geographical unit considered and a slightly more precise one is the economic structure of such a unit, described by the sum of the weighted percentages of people engaged in the four main sectors: agriculture, industry, trade and transportation, and other services.

1.3. Work on related problems

Among the authors already mentioned Bowles concentrates on a different problem, the character of American or Western society and its tendency to perpetuate a certain *class structure*.

Bowles and Gintis [6] find little correlation between IQ and income and suggest that our school system, by attaching so much importance to selection with the aid of IQ, fulfils the function of 'fooling' the population into thinking that an equitable system of sorting them out prevails.

Similarly, Jencks and his collaborators [33] give much attention to the influence of family background, measured by socio-economic status, IQ and education of the individual's parents. In their models a role is also played by the *occupational status* of the future job, a variable which appears to be rather precise, to judge from the high degree of consensus found to exist in various Western societies at different points of time. The role given to this variable in their models has not so far become quite clear; they seem to suggest that in the choice of future job and hence education a fairly important role is played by occupational status aimed at rather than by income expected.

Further Jensen [34] may be quoted who summarized and enriched the literature about '*how to boost IQ*', concentrating on the question of hereditariness of IQ.

In contradistinction to the authors quoted in this section my own concentration was rather on the problem of how *inequality of income can be reduced* and by how much [64, 66] (cf. Chapters 7, 8 and 9). I did not pay attention (except in practical advice to my government) to income from *capital*, partly (as already said) because this is a subject which has been repeatedly analysed by others and partly because in most North-Western European countries a considerable part of this income is taxed to such an extent that the inequality in incomes after tax is predominantly due to inequality in labour income. We might even speak of *exploitation by human capital* as more important today than exploitation by capital in the old sense.

1.4. Differences in material used

Most of the authors mentioned use data on schooling, age, occupation and income, and sometimes add sex, race and economic structure in the limited sense mentioned. These data are available from regular statistical sources, such as population *censuses*, samples therefrom, tax statistics and sometimes education and vital statistics. In addition figures on IQ, parents' IQ, socio-economic status, occupation and income have been used by some of the authors mentioned. These figures have been obtained from special *sample inquiries*, referring to a limited number of individuals investigated in more depth. Whereas the former sources often publish the relationships found between averages for groups of individuals only, the latter often base the relationships shown on the individual data.

With few exceptions, if any, results of regression analysis on *groups* have shown very high correlations, from 0.85 upwards, whereas such analysis applied to *individuals* yields correlations below 0.7, sometimes much below. Clearly in the latter cases some determinants have not been included although they are relevant to the problems dealt with. It cannot be assumed that these lacking variables are highly correlated with those included, because then high correlations would also have been obtained in the research on individuals. Hence the impact of the neglected determinants appears to cancel out in the case of group studies. In agreement with this statement we find that some of the main regression coefficients obtained are roughly the same whether obtained from the study of groups or of individuals. For example the effect of one more year of education on income is found to be $ 240 for 35-year-old individuals in the USA in 1960 as compared to $ 310 for Sweden in 1964, and $ 360 for all ages in the USA in 1960 as compared to a figure of $ 380 for the Netherlands in 1960. It may be even significant that this figure rises with a lower average income of the country considered (cf. also Section 3.5).

1.5. A remark on methods used

As already noted, scientifically the most satisfactory treatment of our problem is one using complete *models*. Models consist of a number of relations each expressing changes in one endogenous variable by one or more other variables supposed to exert a direct influence on that endogenous variable. As an example of the communication gap between disciplines it can be stated that, ignorant of psychological research, econometricians introduced such models around 1936, whereas in psychology such models had been introduced in 1918 under the name of *path analysis* [23]. Thus, as an econometrician, I have been talking path analysis for 38 years without knowing it!

There are some slight differences, though. In their diagrammatic presentation with the aid of an 'arrow scheme' for each direct influence, psychologists are accustomed to using normalized variables (that is, variables transformed so as to have standard deviations of unity) and to noting the partial *regression* coefficient with each arrow. Econometricians do not normally use normalized variables (although it may happen), but are more precise about the *time lags* involved. The latter remark also applies to the models introduced into biology by Volterra [81] referring to the relations between the members of various species (whether as predator and prey or as competitors for the same food, to quote a few examples). In both econometrics and the branch of biology just mentioned, knowledge of the time structure is important for the explanation of cyclic movements in the variables.

1.6. Differences in conclusions

The answers given by various authors, mentioned already or still to be mentioned, to our main question – Can income inequality be reduced? – are widely different. Let me subdivide them into skeptical, not-so-skeptical and optimist answers (cf. Chapter 10).

Skeptical answers have been given by the education planning school and the Jencks group [33]; Jensen probably agrees with the latter [34]. Bowles and Gintis [6] see, as already observed, the class perpetuation as one argument, but also, together with Dougherty [21, 22] and Psacharopoulos [52], the high elasticity of substitution, in production, of one type of labour by other types. A high elasticity of demand corresponds with a low price flexibility, meaning small changes in incomes of different types of labour, even if their relative supply quantities were to change considerably. I tried to show elsewhere that their use of the US census and similar international material can be criticized for not sufficiently identifying demand and supply side. With their own material I find for university-trained vis-à-vis other labour, supply and demand elasticities around unity (negative for demand, positive for supply), a result not far from Freeman's [24]. This is why I do not share their skepticism [70] (cf. also Chapter 5).

The *not-so-skeptical* answers are given also by Burns and Frech [9] and by Ullman [74]. While I have my doubts about the results of the first two authors, their results may be mentioned. They imply that in order to reduce inequality by one-half, average income should be doubled, meaning that Western Europe would have to reach present American income levels. With growth rates around four per cent in income per capita, this could be attained in 18 years.

My own theory, elaborated in Chapter 6, sees the reduction of inequality not as an *automatic* consequence of rising average incomes, but possible only if the expansion of *education overtakes* the expansion required by technological development. Both Ullman and I have collected evidence from which this conclusion can be drawn.

The ratio between qualified and less qualified labour income as defined by Ullman has fallen from 2.50 in 1900 to 1.43 in 1960. On the basis of my theory I forecast that the ratio between income of university graduates and all other labour will fall from 1.9 in 1960 to 1.45 in 1990. For the Netherlands this latter ratio fell from 8.2 in 1900 to 4.6 in 1960 and will continue to fall to 2.9 in 1980 and 2.4 in 1990. The ratio may also be influenced in the future by a *deliberate manipulation of technological development* – a proposition already made for developing countries, but relevant as well for developed countries. With increased awareness of the possibility and desirability of planning technological research somewhat more, rather than leaving it to *laissez-faire*, we may at least explore the extent to which such planning may affect the nature of technological development (cf. Chapters 6, 9).

Too optimistic answers seem to have been given, if I am not misinterpreting them, by some colleagues from Cambridge, Britain. Their theory could be formulated – somewhat exaggerated, admittedly – as considering income distribution the result of an *autonomous political decision* and technology as well as demand for final products as being flexible enough to adapt itself to any income distribution desired. I have not seen any quantitative tests of this theory; but there are some results of previous empirical research which make me doubt very much the truth content of this theory. First, technology of most industries or activities is given within narrow limits of substitution; it is rigid with only a few exceptions (agriculture, building, textiles and handling of materials in any industry). Secondly, the distribution of demand over the main categories of consumer goods and investment goods is inelastic also. High elasticities of substitution have only been found to exist between narrowly related goods, such as Henry Schultz' beef, pork and mutton. So I don't expect the econometric testing of the theory to be successful. Moreover, if it were so easy to freely choose the income distribution, why are the differences in income distribution between Britain and Poland (Wiles and Markowski [83]) so small? And why did the Soviet Union have to make income distribution more unequal in the 1930's?

Looking at the battlefield as a whole I tend to stick to my middle-of-the-road view that we can attain less inequality in a few decades if we let education overtake technology by its supply of more qualified manpower.

There remain other means of attaining less inequality, for example, by *tax* policies. In a number of countries income and wealth taxes can be made more progressive, although hardly so in North-Western Europe – except the tax on capital gains. In a more remote future psychotechnicians may develop a more reliable test battery to estimate an individual's *capabilities*. This may then enable us to use such a test as a tax basis rather than income. By so doing we might open up new possibilities to attain less inequality, since such a tax can be applied as a lump-sum tax (cf. Chapter 8).

2

Trends in income distribution in some Western countries

2.1. Purpose of survey

This chapter tries to present in comparable form a considerable number of figures collected by other authors and by institutions. The figures refer to income distribution in Western countries during the last decades. By way of exception one comparison over a longer period is referred to, and as a contrast some figures on India are given. Income distribution is considered here only as the frequency distribution over households or persons, not as the distribution over factors of production. The purpose of this survey is to remind the reader of the trends in this distribution over the last decades. As is well known, income distribution is one of the important social aspects of our society. Most critics of the 19th and 20th century Western societies have considered income distribution among their criteria. Some of our recent problems, such as wage claims, strikes and inflation, have as a background a continuing dissatisfaction with income distribution and understandably so. The main question behind this survey therefore is: Where do we stand with this important criterion of Western society? This question cannot be answered adequately by only considering primary income distribution. In most countries a considerable degree of redistribution occurs as a consequence of various reforms in the field of taxation, social security and other government intervention.

Even though considerable work has been done in recent decades, the material available shows important lacunae. This implies that for many countries there is scope for undertaking more research in this field. This will be clear from the limited number of countries considered, especially in the tables dealing with redistribution. The phenomenon is of course related to the degree of tax discipline existing in the various countries.

Throughout this essay countries will be indicated by their motor car symbols. For the readers not acquainted with them, they are listed here:

BR	Brazil*	J	Japan*
CDN	Canada	MEX	Mexico*
D	Germany (F.R.)	N	Norway
DK	Denmark	NL	Netherlands
F	France*	RA	Argentina*
GB	United Kingdom	RCH	Chile*
H	Hungary*	S	Sweden
IND	India*	USA	United States

2.2. Some concepts used

Since this author only used material collected by others he did not go into a number of subtleties considered by the original authors. These subtleties are many, especially with regard to the inclusion of some items in or their exclusion from the income concept used. The only concepts used in this study are *primary income* – the income before taxes are paid, *income after tax* and *income after complete redistribution by public finance*. The latter concept includes the imputed values of services rendered to the person or persons considered below cost, minus the amounts actually paid by the recipients. Possible redistribution effects of social insurance institutions of an autonomous character have been neglected. It is often assumed that these redistribution effects are not considerable. For some continental European countries this remains an open question, however.

Among the authors quoted Bentzel [2] explicitly states that

* Countries mentioned occasionally only. Most of the evidence collected refers to countries without an asterisk.

the income-after-complete-redistribution concept he uses equals consumption expenditure, plus savings. Some other sources, namely some of the family budget inquiries and explicitly Dandekar and Rath [18], only collect consumption expenditures; for low incomes the deviation from income will be small.

The main further concepts this study concentrates upon are *income recipients* as different from *households* and *families* and *income per consumer.* By far the larger part of studies quoted deal with one of the first three concepts as their unit of observation; only a small part of them considers the individual consumers as their unit. There is already a difference between households and families, in that most sources do not include single person households as families. Only Nicholson [46] explicitly uses households and families as synonymous. Families may not be identical to income recipients as one family may count more income recipients. Fairly precise information on this aspect is available in many cases. The difference between households and income recipients on the one hand and *persons consuming* on the other hand is much larger, however, than the difference between the number of households and of income recipients. Households of five persons are not exceptional and the average size of households in lower and higher income brackets has developed differently as we shall see (cf. Section 2.6).

The figures collected or calculated from those collected will be shown as much as possible in the form of deciles (tenths) and quintiles (fifths) of the total number of units present in the country and the year studied. It was not always clear how these parts were defined, but as a rule they are parts of the total number of households or of income recipients. All figures of this kind have been expressed as promilles (‰) of total income. In some cases, however, total income has been replaced by median income times total number of incomes, representing something quite different. The only figures not affected by this operation are the ratios between deciles or quintiles, and it is on these that our conclusions concentrate.

2.3. Sources and errors; indicators of inequality

Sources used by the authors quoted may either be 'complete' inquiries, such as census and tax statistics, covering in principle all objects under investigation or 'samples', such as family budgets, sample censuses (cf. [84]) or ad hoc inquiries (for instance, Nicholson [46]). Sampling techniques have advanced sufficiently in order to keep sampling errors under better control than the main source of error: tax evasion. Increased efficiency of tax collection may give some hope that tax evasion is declining; and some checks have been possible, from time to time, to estimate its extent. The increased role of corporations as compared to private firms may also be a favourable development. The subject remains one where more research is highly desirable.

Even though the absolute figures contain considerable errors, the errors in some of the derived figures are considerably less. This applies to comparisons over time, or estimates of the influence of redistribution, which are the main objects of this study.

Several indicators of inequality have been used. The main yardstick used in this survey consists of the ratio between the upper and the lower quintile or the ratio between the upper and the lower decile. They are shown in Tables 2.I.A, 2.II.A, 2.III.A, 2.IV and 2.V. For comparison, in Tables 2.I.B, 2.II.B and 2.III.B some other indicators have been collected. For well-known reasons, Pareto's α has not been used. Those used are:

(i) d, the relative average deviation, that is, the average absolute deviation each income shows from average income, expressed as a portion of average income. Its lower limit is zero (equality of all incomes), its upper limit 2 (a large number of incomes zero and one non-zero).

(ii) P_5, the upper fifth percentile income as a percentage of median income. Of course one could have used other percentiles as well.

(iii) R, the inequality index derived from the Lorenz curve and representing the ratio of the area between the diagonal

Table 2.1.A

Income before taxes for lower and upper deciles or quintiles of income recipients (R), households (H), or families (F); ‰ of total income of country; selected countries and years.

Country	CDN (wages + sal.)		D (R)		DK (R)			GB (R)		
Year	1930/1	1951	1936	1950	1939	1952	1963	1938	1949	1957
Decile 1	–	–	10	10	14	16	–	–	–	–
Decile 2	–	–	20	30	30	32	–	–	–	–
Quintile 1	21	39	30	40	44	48	52	–	72	–
Decile 9	–	–	140	140	158	154	166	120	145	–
Decile 10	–	–	390	340	352	286	260	380	330	280
Quintile 5	485	399	530	480	510	440	426	500	475	–
Source:	[27]		[75]		[3]		[54]	[41]	[75]	[41]

Country	N (sample)		NL (H)			S (R)			USA (F)			
Year	1840	1960	1935	1946	1962	1935	1948[a]	1954[a]	1935/6	1946/7	1959	1960/1
Decile 1	–	–	–	10	15	–	12	20	–	–	–	–
Decile 2	–	–	–	22	30	–	33	36	–	–	–	–
Quintile 1	–	–	59	32	45	–	45	56	41	50	45	46
Decile 9	–	–	–	147	151	166	152	155	–	–	–	–
Decile 10	570	240	366	383	318	395	300	273	517	460	457	455
Quintile 5	–	–	512	530	469	561	452	428	–	–	–	–
Source:	[60]		[82]	[75]	[48]	[2]	[75]	[75]	[28]	[28]	[28]	[7]

[a] Unadjusted tax records.

Table 2.1.B
Other inequality indicators, income before taxes.

(1) Relative average deviation d

Country	GB		NL						USA		
Year	1949	1966	1921	1927	1933	1938	1950	1964	1948	1955	1966
Lower income limit	£ 250	£ 300		Dfl. 1400			Dfl.3000	Dfl.5000	$ 2500	$ 2500	$ 3000
d	0.58	0.48	0.72	0.73	0.65	0.68	0.62	0.48	0.59	0.60	0.45

Source: CBS [11].

(2) Upper 5th percentile income, as a percentage of median (earnings only) P_5

Country	BR	CDN	F	GB	H	J	MEX	RA	RCH	S (all incl.)		USA	
Year[a]		1961								1930	1960	1939	1959
P_5	380	205	280	200	180	280	450	215	400	303	222	267	206

Source: Lydall [42] (only countries for which also indicators of education inequality are given by Lydall).
[a] Years not mentioned; near 1960.

Table 2.1.B (continued)

(3) Inequality index (concentration ratio of Lorenz curve) R, per cent

Country	D		DK		GB		NL		S		Nᵃ		USAᵇ	
Year	1936	1950	1939	1952	1938	1964ᶜ	1938	1962ᶜ	1935	1963ᶜ	1865	1950	1903	1956
R	49	45	50	44	43	40	48	44	54	40	50	32	50	33

Source: UN [75]; N: Soltow [60] p. 55; USA: Keat [36].
ᵃ Average of two towns (Østfold, Vestagter).
ᵇ Wages only.
ᶜ Supplementary information from United Nations.

(4) Maximum equalization percentage E

Country	DK		GB		NL	S	
Year	1939	1965	1938	1955	1950	1935	1948
E	33	27	30	27	31	38	31

Source: UN [75]; DK [54].

and the curve, divided by the area of the triangle under the diagonal. Its limits are 0 (equality) and 1 (a large number of incomes zero and one non-zero).

(iv) *E*, the maximum equalization percentage, being the percentage of total income that must be taken from the higher and given to the lower incomes in order to make them all equal. Also its limits are 0 and 100 per cent.

2.4. Incomes of income recipients, households or families, before taxes

Tables 2.I.A and 2.I.B summarize the information collected from the sources quoted. For Canada the only figures available refer to labour incomes, whereas the other figures cover all incomes. The trend of the lower incomes has been upward and for the highest incomes downward, if expressed in terms of average or median incomes. The most notable exception is the one of the Netherlands in 1935. Partly this may be due to the Great Depression, during which profits were low or negative and a considerable number of households received unemployment benefits; another part of the explanation may be the family size situation, to be discussed in Section 2.6. One more common feature of the figures is that before World War II half of national income went to the 20 per cent highest income recipients, families or households. The Norwegian sample by Soltow is interesting for several reasons. It covers by far the longest period available and shows a clear equalitarian trend, typical for the Scandinavian countries and Britain. Table 2.I.B shows similar features extending also to the Netherlands and the United States and possibly to (Western) Germany.

From Table 2.I.A we derive the following figures on the reduction in inequality as measured by the various indicators (Table 2.I.C).

If the percentage fall of inequality in primary incomes were to last, a reduction to one-half of existing inequality would take 50 to 85 years.

Table 2.I.C
Reduction in inequality.

Indicator	Country	Length of period observed in years	Fall in indicator, per cent	Per cent per year	Average for indicator, per cent per annum
d	GB	17	17	1.0	
	NL	43	33	0.8	1.0
	USA	18	24	1.3	
R	D	14	8	0.6	
	DK	13	12	0.9	
	GB	26	5	0.2	
	NL	22	6	0.3	0.6
	S	28	26	0.9	
	N	85	36	0.4	
	USA	53	34	0.6	
E	DK	26	18	0.7	
	GB	17	10	0.6	0.6
	S	13	7	0.5	

[a] Sample of two towns only.
[b] Wages only.

2.5. Influence of taxes and of complete redistribution

Tables 2.II.A and 2.II.B partly repeat the figures of Tables 2.I.A and 2.I.B, but add income-after-tax figures where they were available. From these tables we note that taxes have reduced the share of the highest decile everywhere and, after World War II, have raised the share of the lowest decile. Since the decile data do not cover many cases, the other indicators, shown in Table 2.II.B, deserve some more attention.

We note that the after-tax inequality index R for Britain fell by 8 percentage points over 21 years, for Denmark by 7 points over 13 years and for Sweden by 11 points over 13 years; the average picture being 9 points in 16 years, hence half a point per annum. If this (linear) trend could go on, the inequality in after-tax incomes could be reduced to half its British value in 1959 during a period of 27 years or one generation. A similar exercise for the maximum equalization percentage E tells us

Table 2.II.A

Income before (B) and after (A) taxes for lower and upper deciles and quintiles of income recipients (R) or families (F); %; ‰ of total income of country; selected countries and years.

Country / Year	DK (R) 1939 B	DK (R) 1939 A	DK (R) 1952 B	DK (R) 1952 A	GB (F)1938 B	GB (F)1938 A	GB (R)1955 B	GB (R)1955 A	GB (F)1957 B	GB (F)1957 A	NL 1946 1950 (R) B	NL 1946 1950 (R) A	NL 1962(F) B	NL 1962(F) A	S (R) 1935 B	S (R) 1935 A	S (R) 1948 B	S (R) 1948 A
Decile 1	14	14	16	17							10	–	28	33				
Decile 2	30	27	32								22	–	47	52				
Quintile 1	44	41	48								32	48	75	85			32	35
Decile 9	158	162	154		120	128	144	149	135	145	147	150	144	145	166	172	163	161
Decile 10	352	350	286	275	380	336	293	245	280	235	383	300	298	251	395	369	303	270
Quintile 5	510	512	440		500	464	437	394	415	380	530	450	439	397	561	541	466	431
Source:	[3]	[75]	[3]	[75]	[41]		[75][76]		[41]		[75][76]		[48]		[75][76]		[75][76]	

Table 2.II.B
Other inequality indicators, income before and after taxes.

(1) Inequality index (Gini ratio of Lorenz curve) R, per cent

Country	DK		GB			NL	S	
Year	1939	1952	1938	1955	1959	1950	1935	1948
R, pre-tax	50	44	43	41	32	45	54	44
R, after-tax	47	40	38	34	30	41	52	41

(2) Maximum equalization percentage E

Country	DK		GB		NL	S	
Year	1939	1952	1938	1955	1950	1935	1948
E, pre-tax	36	31	30	27	31	38	31
E, after tax	34	28	27	24	28	37	28

Source: UN [76]; GB–1959: Nicholson [46].

that in fourteen years a reduction in E by 6 points took place and hence a reduction to half its present value of, say, 20, would take, if the trend continues, 23 years, a comparable figure.

Tables 2.III.A and B show the influence of 'complete redistribution', neglecting possible further redistribution by some autonomous social security institutions. The case of Denmark, based on a very careful inquiry [54] is particularly interesting. The quintile ratio (upper/lower) of 8.2 before tax is reduced to 2 or 3, depending on the assumption made with regard to the profits derived by the various income groups from some of the public overall expenditures. The corresponding figures for the Netherlands are less impressive, but considerable too; one wonders whether the Swedish figures by Bentzel are as comparable as their description suggests [2].

The inequality index R is reduced, according to Table 2.III.B, by 7 percentage points for both the United Kingdom in 1959 and the United States in 1967, corresponding with a reduction

Table 2.III.A

Income before (B) and after (A) complete redistribution, assuming public overhead expenditures to be of equal advantage to (a) each income recipient, (b) in proportion to income received, or (c) either (a) or (b) for various public expenditures.

Country	DK			NL (H)					S			
Year	1963			1935		1962			1935		1948	
Assumption	B	Aa	Ab	B	Ac	B	Aa	Ab	B	A	B	A
Decile 1	.	.	.	.	.	15	21	24	.	.	.	.
Quintile 1	52	132	102	59	70	45	60	65	.	.	32	35
Decile 9	.	126	151	146	145	151	151	150	166	172	163	161
Decile 10	260	140	157	366	315	318	267	242	396	370	301	269
Quintile 5	426	266	308	512	460	469	418	392	562	542	464	430
$\frac{\text{Quintile 5}}{\text{Quintile 1}}$	8.2	2.0	3.0	8.7	6.6	10.4	7.0	6.0	.	.	14.5	12.3
$\frac{\text{Decile 10}}{\text{Decile 1}}$	.	.	.	.	.	21.2	12.7	10.1	.	.	.	.

Source: [54]   [82]   [48]   [2]

Table 2.III.B

Other inequality indicators, income before and after redistribution.

Inequality index (concentration ratio of Lorenz curve) R, per cent

Country	GB		USA
Year	1937	1959	1967
Pre-redistribution	35	32	42
Post-redistribution	27	25	35
Idem, adj. for family size	.	.	31

Source: GB – 1959: Nicholson [46] quoting for 1937 Barna; USA: Lampman [40].

along the trend of about 14 years. The last figure given in Table 2.III.B for the United States will be discussed in Section 2.7.

2.6. Size of households and families

Table 2.IV informs us about an aspect of income distribution not so often discussed, namely the changes over time of the size of households and families in higher and lower income brackets. Over the period for which figures are available, the phenomenon is most pronounced for the Netherlands, where the lower and the upper quintile family size was about equal in 1935/6, but where the ratio upper/lower amounted to 1.77 in 1962. For deciles the change was from 0.79 to 2.05. For households the 1962 ratios are over 3 even.[48]. These figures reflect demographic changes of various kinds. First, family planning in confessional, lower income brackets came late, due to Church resistance. Secondly, both young and old people today can afford to become or remain independent households, which often they could not in the 'thirties or 'twenties.

Similar tendencies can be observed for Germany and Britain, although to a lesser extent, but hardly for the United States according to Selma Goldsmith [28]. Even so average family size is larger in the upper than in the lower quintile. For comparison the figures for India, representing a developing country with as many inhabitants as Africa and Latin America together, have been added. They illustrate the penetration of family planning in the higher income brackets and the virtual absence in the lower income brackets in 1967/8.

2.7. Income ratios for persons in upper and lower strata

Using Table 2.IV we are now able to give a better picture of the trends in income distribution than so far, by calculating ratios of income per capita between high and low family income brackets. It has to be kept in mind that the deciles and quintiles are still based on numbers of households or families and not on numbers of persons in the population. The latter computation can be carried out only with the aid of the base material.

In Table 2.V.A incomes before tax have been shown and, in part B of that table, incomes after complete redistribution.

Table 2.IV

Persons (P) or consumption units (U) per household (H) or family (F) in lower and upper deciles or quintiles; selected countries and years.

Country	D			GB		IND	
	P/H			P/H		P/H	
Year	1927/8	1962/3[a]	1965	1937/9	1957	Rural 1967/8	Urban
Decile 1	3.70	1.81	1.39	3.18	2.00	5.87	6.09
Decile 2	(3.78)	(2.23)	(1.65)	.	.	5.72	6.00
Quintile 1	3.74	2.02	1.52	.	.	5.80	6.05
Decile 9	(3.95)	(3.30)	(3.13)	.	.	4.75	2.89
Decile 10	4.25	3.22	3.13	3.54	4.45	4.20	2.50
Quintile 5	4.10	3.14	3.13	.	.	4.48	2.70
Quintile 5 / Quintile 1	1.10	1.55	2.06	.	.	0.77	0.45
Decile 10 / Decile 1	1.15	1.78	2.25	1.29	2.23	0.71	0.41
Source:	[56]	[29]	[84]	[17]	[46]	[18]	

Country	NL					USA			
	U/F		P/F		P/H	P/F			
Year	1923/4[b]	1935/6[b]	1935/6	1962	1962	1903	1935/6	1941	1959
Decile 1	(3.30)	(3.76)	5.35	2.40	1.21	.	.	.	.
Quintile 1	(3.58)	(3.18)	4.50	2.58	1.39	3.48	3.73	3.55	3.24
Decile 5	(3.20)	(3.36)	4.20	4.99	4.63	.	.	.	.
Quintile 5	(3.78)	(3.60)	4.60	4.82	4.50	3.86	3.92	4.00	3.89
Quintile 5 / Quintile 1	(1.05)	(1.13)	1.02	1.77	3.23	1.11	1.05	1.12	1.20
Decile 10 / Decile 1	(0.97)	(0.89)	0.79	2.05	3.82	.	.	.	.
Source:	[8]	[10]	[10]	[48]	[48]	[39]	[28]	[28]	[28]

[a] Hamburg only.
[b] Amsterdam only.

Table 2.V
Ratios of income between upper and lower groups; quintiles (Q) or deciles (D) per household (H) or family (F) compared with ratios per person (P), using assumptions (a), (b) or (c) on advantage of public expenditures for various groups (cf. Table 2.III).

A. Highest to lowest ratios of income before tax

Country	D		NL		USA	
Year	H Prewar[a]	H Postwar[b]	H 1935/6	H 1962	F 1935/6	F 1959
Q ratio H or F	17.7	12.0	8.7	10.4	12.6	9.9
Q ratio P	16.1	5.6	8.5	3.2	12.0	8.2
D ratio H or F	.	34	.	31	.	.
D ratio P	.	15	.	5.5	.	.

Source : Tables 2.I and 2.IV.
[a] Incomes : 1936; household size : 1927/8.
[b] Incomes : 1950; household size : 1965.

B. Highest to lowest ratio of income (quartile or decile averages) after complete redistribution per household (H), family (F) and per person (P)

Country	NL				
Year	H[a] 1935/6	H 1962		F[b] 1962	
Assumption[c]	c	a	b	a	b
Q ratio H or F	6.6	7.0	6.0	7.0	6.0
Q ratio P	6.4	2.2	1.9	4.0	3.4
D ratio H or F	.	12.7	10.1	.	.
D ratio P	.	3.3	2.6	.	.

Source : Tables 2.III and 2.IV.
[a] H for incomes.
[b] F for family size.
[c] Cf. Table 2.III.

For recent years the figures per capita for the new countries where data have been found are considerably more favourable than the figures for households or families. In Germany they are reduced to one-half, in the Netherlands to one-third; in the United States the reduction, as expected, is less. For incomes per capita after complete redistribution quintile ratios are now obtained comparable to the Danish figures in Table 2.III.A. The American figure for *R* in 1967 in Table 2.III.B, after adjustment for family size, is in line with those for 1959 in Table 2.V.A.

No figures for Scandinavian countries were found; to the extent that the Dutch changes between 1935/6 and 1962 are due to the belated penetration of family planning into lower income groups, changes over the last decades may have been not so outspoken in these countries.

Again for comparison, figures have been added for consumption expenditure in India (Table 2.VI). The differences with Western countries are striking and reflect the dramatic problems of developing countries in social matters.

Table 2.VI

Some data on consumption expenditure in rupees per person per annum in lower and upper income brackets; 1960/1 and 1967/8 (constant 1960/1 prices); rural (R) and urban (U) areas and ratios.

Year	1960/1		1967/8	
	R	U	R	U
Decile 1	88.0	113.0	88.4	95.3
Decile 2	100.4	156.1	102.0	145.1
Quintile 1	188.4	269.1	190.4	241.0
Decile 9	382.5	553.5	399.2	580.2
Decile 10	682.0	1061.1	711.7	1054.9
Quintile 5	1064.5	1614.6	1110.9	1635.1
$\dfrac{\text{Decile 10}}{\text{Decile 1}}$	7.8	9.4	8.1	11.0
$\dfrac{\text{Quintile 5}}{\text{Quintile 1}}$	5.7	6.0	5.8	6.8

Source : Dandekar and Rath [18].

2.8. Summary

Although the material available shows well-known lacunae and uncertainties, errors in changes over time and in the estimation of the effects of redistribution schemes will be less than errors in the absolute figures. Our main findings are:

(1) The trend in income shares of the lowest groups over the last decades has been upward, that of the highest groups downward (Table 2.I.A).

(2) If the observed percentage reduction of inequality per year were to last it would take 50 to 85 years in order to reduce existing inequality to one-half (Tables 2.I.B and 2.I.C).

(3) Taxes have reduced the after-tax income share of the highest decile and raised, after World War II, the share of the lowest decile (Table 2.II.A).

(4) If the linear trend in inequality indicators for incomes after tax were to continue, halving inequality would take some 25 years or one generation (Table 2.II.B).

(5) Complete redistribution by public finance reduces the ratio of the upper to the lower quintile from 8 to 2.5 in Denmark (1963) and from 14 to 6.5 in the Netherlands (1962) (Table 2.III.A).

(6) If the trend in *R* for incomes after complete redistribution were to continue, reduction to one-half of its present value would take 14 years (Section 2.5).

(7) Demographic factors have improved income distribution over persons more than over families (Table 2.IV), especially in the Netherlands.

(8) For the Netherlands in 1962 the ratio of *income per capita* for the upper to the lower family income quintile is 2 as compared to 6.5 for *income per household;* contrast this with the situation in 1935/6 when there was no difference between this ratio for per capita income and income per household. Similar changes took place in Germany and in Britain (Tables 2.IV and 2.V), but to a lesser extent.

(9) In India the ratios of consumption expenditures per capita of high incomes to low incomes are high and have increased between 1960/1 and 1967/8 (Table 2.VI), illustrating the dramatic social situation there.

3

Some examples of 'price equations'

3.1. Theory and terminology used

In this book incomes are considered to be *prices* paid for various types of production factors, mainly labour of different qualifications. Capital incomes, having been discussed by many authors, are only touched upon occasionally (cf. Chapter 9). Our emphasis will be on the *compartments of the labour market* which in principle can be characterized by any number of aspects and by the *degrees* to which these aspects have to be present. Often the aspect of *years of schooling* will be used and a distinction will then be made between schooling *required* for the jobs in the compartment and *available* schooling. This implies that already this single aspect gives rise to two indicators or indexes needed to identify the compartment.

Let us first consider one single compartment and the price prevailing in it. Applying customary economic theory we will try to explain that price by the interaction between demand and supply. This implies that two relationships are being introduced, known as the *supply equation* and the *demand equation*. Both contain the price and the quantities 'bought' and 'sold'; the latter two are supposed to be identical and will be called the 'employment' of the labour type considered. As a rule the relations also contain other variables. Those occurring in the supply equation are usually called *supply factors*, and those occurring in the demand equation, *demand factors*. In a model describing one single market, price and employment will be considered to be the endogenous variables and the supply and demand factors to be the exogenous variables of the model. Solving for the two endogenous variables we obtain what we will call the *price equation* and the *employment equation*. The former expresses the price and the latter expresses employment in terms of supply and demand factors. These two equations may also be called the *reduced forms* of the market equations.

So far our considerations about a single compartment. However, our interest is in income *distribution*, in the distribution of prices and employment volumes among the various compartments. For a small number of compartments income distribution may be described by a list of all price and employment equations. A clearer picture of distribution will be obtained, however, by choosing a smaller number of *inequality measures*, especially when a large number of compartments is being studied. A large number of inequality measures are currently being used. The simplest among them are one or more ratios or differences between prices. More complicated ones are such concepts as the standard deviation of the price distribution, where employment figures are the frequencies, or the Lorenz inequality coefficient shown in Chapter 2. In a general way we may state that inequality measures are obtained by applying some operator to prices and employment figures; and with the aid of price and employment equations, the result will be expressed in terms of corresponding functions of supply and demand factors. In the simplest cases these functions will be measures of the level and distribution of supply and demand factors.

In the subsequent sections three examples will be given of this approach, tailored to the data made available by Lydall [42], Chiswick [16] and Soltow [60], all of them supplemented with additional data from other sources.

3.2. A cross-section test with national figures

The test to be discussed here is applied to income distribution figures published by Lydall [42] and referring to the ratio of the fifth percentile (from the top) to the median of Lydall's standard income distribution, where only earnings have been considered. This implies an underestimation of income inequality, although less so than many think: in developed countries three-quarters of primary income inequality (and much more of income-after-tax inequality) is due to labour income inequality.

The measure chosen for the only supply factor considered consists of *enrolment* in primary and secondary schools as a percentage of the age group from 5–19 years. A high enrolment figure is supposed to affect inequality negatively since it raises competition for qualified and lowers competition for unqualified labour. Alternatively, inequality in schooling, expressed by its Lorenz coefficient in a 1971 publication by Chiswick [15], has been introduced. As a second alternative, higher education enrolment per 1000 aged 20–29 has been used.

Demand distribution has been represented alternatively by the percentage of the economically active population in manufacturing, by the adult male labour in agriculture as a percentage of total male labour and by GNP per capita. The philosophy behind these alternative dummy variables is that more industrialized, or less agrarian, or simply richer countries will demand relatively more qualified labour. In the next section this idea will be pursued further and refined.

In this chapter differences between the technological level of countries or American states have been neglected. This subject will be taken up in Chapters 5 and 6.

One further experiment suggested in Chiswick's study [15] has been undertaken, namely the addition as an explanatory variable of the rate of growth of GNP per capita.

Table 3.1 shows some of the results obtained.

Before discussing some of my results I want to point out that, unfortunately, many of the regression coefficients found are highly *unstable*, depending on the choice of further explanatory variables or due, sometimes, to multicollinearity among the explanatory variables. In some cases this can be avoided by introducing *a priori* values or ratios of values for the regression

Table 3.I

Some regression equations obtained from cross-section tests explaining income inequality x; R = correlation coefficient, corrected for degrees of freedom.

No.	Regression coefficient for (· not included)								R̄	Theory[a]	No. of countries included	Source :
	y	y'	z	u	v	w	w'	$\dot{w}'$				
1	−4.4	0.34					−0.016	87.3	0.75	Chiswick	9	Lydall [42]
2	−3.6		−1.1						0.72	Lydall	15	UNRISD [77]
3									0.64	Lydall	15	Chiswick [15]
4	−1.74			−5.85		−0.019			0.82	Tinbergen	15	UNRISD [77]
5	−2.24			−6.23					0.78	Tinbergen	15	UNRISD [77]
6	−3.36					−0.031			0.74	Lydall	15	Lydall [42]
7	−0.89		−1.3	−6.31	+1.72				0.76	Tinbergen	15	UNRISD [77]
8	−0.42								0.54	Lydall	15	UNRISD [77]
9	−4.6[b]			+2.3[b]					0.58	Tinbergen	17	Chiswick [15]
												Chiswick [15]

a Cf. text.
b Ratio of coefficients, chosen on a priori grounds, 2 : −1.

Symbol definition :

x :   Fifth percentile, as per cent of median of 'standard income distribution' (Lydall).
y :   Enrolment (combined primary and secondary) as per cent of age group 5–19 years (indicator 23).
y' :   Lorenz coefficient of schooling, in per mille.
z :   Higher education enrolment per 1000 aged 20–29 (indicator 27).
u :   Per cent economically active population in manufacturing (ISIC divisions 2,3) (indicator 55).
v :   Adult male labour in agriculture as per cent of total male labour (ISIC division 0) (indicator 50).
w :   GNP per capita (1959/61), in 1960 US $, at parity rate (indicator 69).
w' :   Average per capita GNP in 1967 prices for 1950/60.
$\dot{w}'$:   Percentage change in GNP per capita in constant 1967 prices (dollar equivalent) from 1950 to 1960.

coefficients for some variables. For the testing of my own theory this is possible, for instance, if demand for and supply of some type of qualified labour are expressed in the same units, for instance, percentages of active population.

From Table 3.I we may conclude that all cases shown are unanimous about the algebraic sign of the level of education: it is negative, meaning that more education will reduce income inequality. The order of magnitude does not vary too much either, except in equation 8, where the inclusion of v (percentage in agriculture), inspired by one of Lydall's suggestions, takes over the role of y but yields a poor correlation. The influence of u (percentage in manufacturing) appears remarkably stable, except where a positive sign has been imposed (following my own theory), but with hardly more success than Lydall's case. Where two variables of the level of education (y and z) have been introduced, the relative influence of each is open to doubt but the joined influence less so. Wherever the variable u has been introduced freely, it obtains the wrong sign from my point of view and takes over part of the influence of education.

In order to answer the question of what increase in education will be needed to reduce income inequality in the socially more advanced countries to one-half of its present level, we have to insert $\Delta x = -50$. The answer will depend on the relative change in higher (z) as compared to 'lower' (y) education. Assuming that only a portion of those who receive more 'lower' education – we assume 6 per cent – will be able to follow higher education, we have $\Delta z = 0.6\Delta y$. The results for Δy and Δz (when considered) are found in Table 3.II.

In order to appraise the feasibility of the changes found, we must compare these changes to the actual figures already attained. The highest figures for primary and secondary education enrolment given by UNRISD are 81 for the USA, Canada and Belgium; Sweden and Denmark show 69 and 71, respectively, Germany (F.R.) 72, the Netherlands 75, France 76. Some of the changes shown in Table 3.II are impossible, therefore, while others seem to be *within reach*. Enrolment for higher education is, of course, quite a bit lower.

Table 3.II
Increase in education enrolment needed to reduce
income inequality by one-half.

Equation	$\Delta y\,(\%)$	$\Delta z\,(\%_0)$
2	11	.
3	12	7
4	29	.
5	22	.
6	15	.
7	30	18
8	33	20
9	11	.

3.3. Two time series tests

Another test was based on time series data available for the Netherlands and Norway; the latter country is represented by a sample studied by Soltow [60]. Indicators available for income distribution and supply and demand factors have been given the same main symbols as in the preceding set of computations, but with a varying number of primes. Table 3.III shows the results.

Again we may ask what change in education is needed in order to reduce to one-half the income inequality of 1960. For the Netherlands this means $\Delta x'' = -0.3$. Assuming that in the future almost 90% of the population will have secondary education ($\Delta z' = 500$), we find that $\Delta z'' = 54$, which means that enrolment in higher education should be *doubled* in comparison to the present situation. For Norway we find that $\Delta x''' = -16$ requires also *doubling* z''' (from 32.10^{-5} in 1960 to 64.10^{-5}). In Norway so far z''' has doubled every thirty years. In considering these provisional results we should remember that their margin of error is very large.

Apart from education some other of the explanatory variables may also be partly or indirectly considered as action parameters. Thus, Chiswick's equation 1 (Table 3.I) suggests that a country's *rate of growth* exerts an influence on income distribution. With a lower rate of growth income distribution

Table 3.III

Time series tests based on a demand–supply theory; corrected correlation coefficient.

Country	Period	Regression equation	$\bar{R}$
Netherlands	1920–1960	$x'' = 0.6 + 0.00199u' - 0.00043z'$ $- 0.00156z''$	0.78
Norway	1875–1950	$x''' = 43.8 - 20.000\,\dfrac{z'''}{u''} + 0.016\,p$	0.90

Definition of symbols :   *Source :*

Netherlands

x''	Relative average absolute deviation (of individual incomes from average income)	CBS [11]
z'	Enrolment in secondary and scientific education per 1000 of age groups concerned	CBS [13]
z''	Enrolment in scientific education per 1000 of age group	CBS [13]
u'	Active population in manufacturing (weight 1) and services (weight 3) per 1000	CBS [13]

Norway

x'''	Gini coefficient of income inequality, Østfold and Vestagter (for 1960 Østfold only)	Soltow [60]
z'''	Number of students passing final university exam divided by total population	Norges HS [47]
u''	Percentage of active population outside primary industries	Norges HS [47]
p	Ratio of wealth to income	Soltow [60]

will be less unequal. A reduction by 50 points in x, meaning, as I said, halving the inequality of the socially advanced countries, will be obtained if the *rate of growth of income* per capita is reduced by 0.6 per cent. The other measures used in Chiswick's article [15] for income inequality [Lydall's P(10) and P(75)], when halved, would require, according to the corresponding equations, reductions in growth rates of 1.4 and 0.8 per cent, that is, figures of the same order. The reader should again be reminded of the sensitivity of the coefficients to the inclusion of other explanatory variables.

The same equation suggests that a reduction of inequality to one-half of its existing value could be obtained by an *increase in per capita GNP* of $ 3000, or by more than doubling the 1960 American GNP per capita. I already pointed out that a difference of opinion exists among the authors discussed, even about the direction of a change in income 'needed'; this can be demonstrated with the aid of some material to which I will return in the next section.

3.4. Cross-section studies for parts of countries*

3.4.1. Introduction

Three studies by Americans, namely T. Paul Schultz [58], Leland S. Burns and H. E. Frech III [9], and Barry R. Chiswick [16] which are based on an interesting and large amount of information, are the basis for the present section. Some material selected and processed by the present author is also included.

The data pertains to subdivisions of three countries: the United States, Canada, and the Netherlands. Although the authors mentioned adhere to theories of income distribution somewhat different from my demand–supply theory [63], their material can also be used to test the latter, subject to some assumptions. The material added by my own modest extension seems to fit the purpose somewhat better, however. One of the points of focus of this section therefore consists of attempts to give practical shape to the introduction of variables supposed to represent demand. These attempts will be followed by still others in Section 3.5.

One condition to be fulfilled for any attempt to test the demand–supply theory is that the geographical units compared in a cross-section or time series analysis be *large enough* to contain both the demand and the supply location. For commuters there is a distinction between the place where they work (and where the demand is exerted) and the place where

* I want to express my sincere thanks to my collaborators A. ten Kate and H. Visscher for programming many of the calculations used in this section.

the supply is shown). This implies that cross-section studies using single municipalities, such as the Burns–Frech study and some of T. P. Schultz's investigations, may lead to unreliable results. For that reason I have preferred to use data for only the (eleven) provinces of the Netherlands, as was also done by Schultz.

As already mentioned, this section deals with cross-section analyses for three countries. The figures refer to the states of the United States (Chiswick), the provinces of Canada (same author) and a number of municipalities (Burns and Frech), the socio-geographic areas and the provinces of the Netherlands (Schultz, Tinbergen). Burns and Frech, in particular, chose the 71 largest municipalities, Schultz 88 selected at random, and both Schultz and I took the eleven provinces of my country. The advantage of the type of material chosen consists of homogeneity in cultural and other respects, partly unknown even, which does not exist in cross-section studies among widely differing countries as carried out by Lydall [42] and in Section 3.2. This homogeneity is also lacking in time series studies because of changes both in the system of education and in the technology of production.

There are also disadvantages connected with cross-section studies within a single country; one has been mentioned already: commuters do not always work and live in the same geographical unit. Another is that variations of variables within one country, especially a small country, may be so restricted as to be a hindrance to extrapolations, which are the main instruments for arriving at the more interesting answers we want to derive from our studies.

The variables used in this subsection have been listed in Table 3.IV. Except for the last column the demand index used was the average income of the geographical units considered. Schultz did not use this variable. In Subsection 3.4.5 the better demand index Y'' will be used for the Netherlands and similar data for the United States will be used in Section 3.5.

Table 3.IV

List of variables used by the authors quoted (USA = United States of America; CDN = Canada; NL = Netherlands).

Symbol	USA and CDN	NL		
	Chiswick	Schultz	Burns and Frech	Tinbergen
X	X : Variance of nat. logs of income in \$ 1000	X'' : Concentr. ratio of income	X'' : Concentr. ratio of income	X'' : Highest decile of income
Y	Y : Average of nat. logs of income in \$ 1000	*	Y'' : Income in Dfl. 1000	Y'' : Demand index[c]
Z	Z : Average number of years of schooling for males over 25	Z'' : Males 40–64 : % with higher education[a]	Z'' : Years of schooling[b]	Z''' : Per cent of active population with secondary and higher education
U	U : Variance in number of years of schooling for males over 25	*	U'' : Concentr. ratio of schooling	U'' : Per cent of active population with higher education
V	V : Nat. log of Y_0 (income at zero schooling)	*	*	*

Note: Capital letters are used for variables in units indicated; lower case letters will be used for 'normalized' variables (i.e., average = 0, standard deviation = 1). Asterisk means : variable not used.

[a] For 1960 : percentage of active males with higher education.
[b] Total population.
[c] Defined in Section 3.4.5.

3.4.2. Using Chiswick's material for the United States

For each of the data collections analysed we used two ways of measuring the variables used: the 'natural units' as indicated in Table 3.IV, and the normalized units (with zero average and unit standard deviation), the latter being indicated by lower case letters. We attempted to study the structure of relationships by comparing regression coefficients for the same variable in different combinations with other variables. Chiswick's material on the USA was used for Table 3.V.

Table 3.V

Regression and multiple correlation coefficients R found for different combinations of variables explaining income inequality x.

No.	Regression coefficients for				R	
	y	z	u	v		
1	−0.79	.	.	.	0.79	
2	.	−0.73	.	.	0.73	1 expl. var.
3	.	.	+0.48	.	0.48	
4	.	.	.	−0.86	0.86	
5	−0.60	−0.23	.	.	0.80	
6	−0.71	.	+0.25	.	0.825	2 expl. var.
7	+0.08	.	.	−0.94	0.86	
8	−0.82	+0.15	+0.31	.	0.83	
9	+1.25	−0.67	.	−1.58	0.93	3 expl. var.
10	+0.65	.	+0.42	−1.38	0.94	
11	+1.02	−0.33	+0.315	−1.52	0.94	4 expl. var.

Source: [16] Table 3-3.

We did not use all the variables shown in Chiswick's study, for instance not his variable $\hat{r}$, the rate of return on education derived per state from the regression, in that state, of income on schooling. My feeling is that its use duplicates the variables Z and U, since Chiswick's (and Mincer's) theory is that everybody's choice of length of schooling is partly based on $\hat{r}$. It seems that indeed $\hat{r}$ is superfluous, even statistically; there appears to be complete multicollinearity in the set $(x, y, z, u, v, \hat{r})$.

The following conclusions seem warranted:
The influence exerted by variables *u* (education inequality) and *v* (representing other influences on income, such as innate capabilities) are stable; variable *v* always raises considerably the correlation coefficient. The contribution of *u* is less important, but stable. The influence of *y*, taken here to represent the demand for qualified manpower, looks uncertain since positive as well as negative regression coefficients are found. Negative coefficients occur when and only when *v* is excluded. The cases with the highest multiple correlation coefficients show a positive regression coefficient for *y*. The influence exerted by variable *z* is negative in most cases. These statements induce me to select case no. 11 as the most satisfactory relationship found with the aid of Chiswick's material.

To obtain natural units we must divide the corresponding symbols by their standard deviations, given below (Source: [16] Table G-5): $\sigma_x = 0.12$; $\sigma_y = 0.23$; $\sigma_z = 0.79$; $\sigma_u = 3.17$; $\sigma_v = 0.29$; the relation then becomes

$$X = 0.532Y - 0.050Z + 0.012U - 0.629V. \qquad (3.1)$$

As an *illustration* of the influence which a higher level and a more equal distribution of education may exert, we assume an increase in years of schooling of 2 and a reduction of its variance of 4; such changes would lead to $\Delta X = -0.100 - 0.048 = -0.148$. Since the average value of *X*, that is $\overline{X} = 0.79$, this represents a very modest reduction of inequality in income in the United States; it *reduces the standard deviation of incomes* from $\sqrt{0.790}$ to $\sqrt{0.642}$ or from 0.89 to 0.80 or *by only 10 per cent*. As we shall see in the case of the Netherlands, the coefficients for *Z* and *U* may become larger, however, if *Y* is replaced by a better measure for demand.

3.4.3. Using Chiswick's material for Canada

Chiswick has collected for Canada the same material as for the USA. Some of the results obtained with its aid are given in Table 3.VI. Here we see that the influence exerted by *y* and

Table 3.VI

Regression and multiple correlation coefficients R found for different combinations of variables explaining x.

No.	Regression coefficients for				R	
	y	z	u	v		
1	−0.62	.	.	.	0.62	
2	.	−0.54	.	.	0.54	1 expl. var.
3	.	.	−0.15	.	0.15	
4	.	.	.	−0.67	0.67	
5	−0.55	−0.09	.	.	0.625	
6	−0.85	.	+0.38	.	0.68	2 expl. var.
7	+0.08	.	.	−0.74	0.67	
8	−1.93	+0.90	+0.91	.	0.76	
9	+1.17	−0.49	.	−1.48	0.72	3 expl. var.
10	+0.59	.	+0.82	−1.83	0.86	
11	+0.10	+0.27	+0.92	−1.61	0.86	4 expl. var.

Source : [16] Table 3-12.

z is unstable, whereas that exerted by u and v is relatively stable. Also, inclusion of u or v considerably raises the correlation coefficient. Transforming equation 11 into one with the units used by Chiswick and mentioned in Table 3.I, we obtain

$$\frac{X}{0.09} = 0.10\frac{Y}{0.21} + 0.27\frac{Z}{0.78} + 0.92\frac{U}{1.08} - 1.61\frac{V}{0.26},$$

or

$$X = 0.043Y + 0.031Z + 0.077U - 0.56V. \tag{3.2}$$

In contrast to the result for the United States, there is a positive influence of the average level Z of education on income inequality X; this implies that the average level may already be too high. A possible explanation may be in the fact that in Canada education is obligatory to a larger extent than in the United States; at least for Great Britain this argument is used by Chiswick [14] and in this respect Canada is probably somewhat closer to Britain than the United States.

Considering that $\overline{U} = 10.69$, we may think of a reduction in the inequality of schooling as a means to reduce income inequality and estimate the influence of $\Delta U = -5$. This would mean that the standard deviation in years of schooling is reduced from $\sqrt{10.69}$ to $\sqrt{5.69}$ or from 3.27 years to 2.39 years. We obtain

$$\Delta X = -0.385. \tag{3.3}$$

Since $\overline{X} = 0.63$, this brings inequality as measured by X to less than one-half of its present value; but when measured as a standard deviation in the natural logarithms of income it falls from $\sqrt{0.63}$ to $\sqrt{0.245}$ or from 0.794 to 0.495, a *reduction by 38 per cent only.*

A common feature of the equation found for both the United States and Canada is that raising the Y_0, which stands for the factors other than schooling which determine an individual's productivity, reduces inequality in about the same way. This may in part reflect the influence of the 'environment', including the influence of the education of the parents. If this interpretation is correct, the long-run influence of education may be considerably stronger than the direct influence estimated.

3.4.4. *Research on the Netherlands by T.P. Schultz and by L.S. Burns – H.E. Frech III*

Schultz's contributions [58] to the explanation of income inequality (p. 352) consist of having assembled a vast collection of statistical data, for 11 provinces, for 75 regions, and for 88 municipalities selected in a random sample (pp. 339/340) and of having analysed various relations in order to explain changes over time with the aid of various explanatory variables. He has also studied cross-section data. For this publication the latter are the more relevant analyses. Income inequality among regions as well as among provinces, as measured by their concentration ratios, has been explained by a variety of variables, including the level of education, for which Schultz found a positive influence. No use is made of demand factors, which prevents us from testing the demand–supply theory. The other explanatory variables include the number of tax-payers, unemployment and wealth. The best results are obtained for the most recent year studied by him, 1958, and for the provinces. This seems to confirm the viewpoint that the geographical units should not be chosen too small. With the aid of the education level (measured as the percentage of active population having had higher education) a corrected correlation coefficient of 0.89 is obtained. This result comes close to my own results, to be discussed in Section 3.4.5.

Burns and Frech used the figures for 71 of the larger municipalities. Their material enabled me to compute Table 3.VII, where the symbols are those explained in Table 3.IV.

Table 3.VII

Regression and multiple correlation coefficients R found for different combinations of variables explaining income inequality x'.

No.	Regression coefficients for			R	
	y'	z''	u'		
1	− 0.91	.	.	0.91	1 expl. var.
2	.	− 0.50	.	0.50	
3	.	.	− 0.68	0.68	
4	− 0.92	+ 0.02	.	0.91	2 expl. var.
5	− 1.05	.	+ 0.175	0.91	
6	− 1.04	− 0.02	+ 0.177	0.91	3 expl. var.

Source : [9] Table 1b, and figures on z'' kindly supplied by the authors.

These results may be interpreted so as to attach the main role in the explanation to *income*, with a clearly *negative* influence. The influence of the two education variables is secondary, with that of the level of education uncertain as to its algebraic sign, whereas inequality of education shows a positive influence. If income y' can be considered as a demand indicator for high qualification, its influence should be positive. This interpretation leads to a rejection of the demand–supply theory. But I have some doubts, already announced, whether the geographical units are not too small. A group of typically commuter municipalities, whose commuters work in the nearby large cities of Amsterdam, Rotterdam and The

Hague, do not reflect the demand for the commuters' qualifications. The municipalities happen to have high incomes and at the same time low inequality of incomes. In the next section we will find that for the larger units, the provinces, a completely different situation prevails.

3.4.5. *Further research on the Netherlands*

In an attempt to test the demand–supply theory I tried to construct a slightly more precise indicator for demand. From the American 1960 Census of Population quoted in [58] the percentage of manpower with higher education was found for the four main sectors: agriculture, manufacturing, trade and transportation, and services (defined as the remainder). For each of the Dutch provinces the total number of persons active in the four main sectors are known from the Dutch 1960 Census of Population. Multiplying the percentage with the higher education needed, as taken from American figures, a (probably overestimated) *index of demand* was derived. On the supply side, two indicators were used, in order to open up the possibility of different weights being given to manpower with secondary and to manpower with third-level higher education. At the same time it was assumed that the private cost of third-level education is related to income foregone, to be represented by a constant, reflecting the income of people with only secondary education.

The demand–supply theory was given a shape better adapted to the data available. As the variable representing income inequality we considered the upper decile income divided by average income (in Lydall's [42] notation P_{10}). Demand for and supply of people with higher education were represented by $d_1 + d_2$ and $s_1 + s_2$, respectively, where the indices 1 and 2 represent two subgroups: group 2 being university graduates and group 1 representing all other people with higher education. As set out in Section 2, the differences between demand and supply were taken as two explanatory variables, but the possibility was kept open that the weights of the two differences

$d_1 - s_1$ and $d_2 - s_2$ could be different: a scarcity in category 2 may be more important to explain inequality than the same scarcity in category 1. Taking into account that in the absence of inequality X'' must be 1 and that our method of calculating quantities demanded is based on American figures, a formula of the following shape was tested:

$$X'' = \xi_1(d_1 - s_1) + \xi_2(d_2 - s_2) + 1 + c, \qquad (3.4)$$

where c indicates the correction for the use of American figures. The data available do not permit us to introduce d_1 and d_2 separately, however. For this reason we combine $\xi_1 d_1 + \xi_2 d_2$ to $\xi Y''$ and specify the correction term c to be $\xi(\bar{Y}'' - \bar{Y}_o'')$, where the suffix o refers to the United States. Replacing s_1 and s_2 by $Z''' - U''$ and U'' (cf. Table 3.IV), respectively, we finally obtain, for the purpose of testing the demand–supply theory,

$$X'' = \xi Y'' - \xi_1(Z''' - U'') - \xi_2 U'' + 1 + \xi(\bar{Y}'' - Y_o'').$$

Our best result obtained runs

$$X'' = 1.21 Y'' - 0.08 Z''' - 1.16 U'' - 11.4$$

$$(R = 0.96). \qquad (3.5)$$

This is equivalent to putting $\xi = 1.21$; $\xi_1 = 0.08$ and $\xi_2 = 1.24$. This would leave us with an estimate of $\bar{Y}'' - \bar{Y}_o'' = -10.3$. The direct estimate of the percentage of active population with higher education in both countries yields

$$\bar{Y}'' = 10.4; \qquad \bar{Y}_o'' = 19.1,$$

implying a value for $\bar{Y}'' - Y_o'' = -8.7$. In order to test the stability of the regression coefficients found, we constructed Table 3.VIII, comparable with Tables 3.V, 3.VI and 3.VII, using normalized variables.

The negative influence of the supply variables and the positive influence of the demand variable is confirmed by cases 4 and 5.

In order to compare these results with those for the two

Table 3.VIII
Regression and multiple correlation coefficients R found for different combinations of variables explaining income inequality x''.

No.	Regression coefficients for			R	
	y''	z'''	u''		
1	0.84	.	.	0.84	⎫
2	.	0.81	.	0.81	⎬ 1 expl. var.
3	.	.	0.70	0.70	⎭
4	1.03	−0.20	.	0.845	⎫ 2 expl. var.
5	2.50	.	−1.72	0.95	⎭
6	2.95	−0.42	−1.75	0.96	3 expl. var.

Table 3.IX
Regression and multiple correlation coefficients R found for different combinations of explanatory variables explaining x''.

No.	Regression coefficients for			R
	y	z'''	u''	
1	0.88	.	.	0.88
2	.	0.81	.	0.81
3	.	.	0.70	0.70
4	0.92	−0.04	.	0.88
5	1.02	.	−0.17	0.88
6	0.89	+0.27	−0.31	0.89

Table 3.X
Regression and multiple correlation coefficients R found for different combinations of variables explaining x'.

No.	Regression coefficients for			R
	y''	z'''	u''	
1	0.92	.	.	0.92
2	.	0.89	.	0.89
3	.	.	0.90	0.90
4	0.87	−0.055	.	0.92
5	0.91	.	+0.092	0.92
6	0.89	−0.054	+0.083	0.92

other countries and those obtained by Burns and Frech for the Netherlands (based on municipalities), we constructed similar tables for a few alternative variables, using y' instead of y'' (closer to Chiswick's material) for Table 3.IX and x' instead of x'' (Burns and Frech) for Table 3.X.

The results presented in the last two tables are less satisfactory than those of Table 3.VIII: the multiple correlation coefficients are lower and the supply influences are small and uncertain.

3.4.6. Some preliminary conclusions

The only case, in the present section, where a considerable influence of the level and the inequality of education on income distribution is found, is equation (3.5). In order to reduce income inequality, as measured by the highest decile divided by average income, to half of its 1960 value, that is, in order to attain $\Delta X = -2$, we need $\Delta U'' = 2/1.24 = 1.61$, meaning that the percentage of the population with university education should be more than doubled in comparison to the 1960 situation, when it was 1.4 per cent. Such favourable results were found in several other cases reported in Chapter 2; but most of the present results are much less favourable in that sense. From the various versions of the relationship found for the Netherlands one may wonder whether perhaps the use of the demand indicator as defined in Section 3.4.5 might not change the American and Canadian figures so as to show a stronger influence of education level or distribution on income inequality.* This will be undertaken in Section 3.5.

Another conclusion seems to be that municipalities are too small as units to compare to each other because of the different 'location' of demand and supply in our sense.

In a last attempt to compare our cross-section analyses we

---

* It is also conceivable that a longer-term influence on income distribution may be implicit in the influence of variable V, as already observed in Section 5. This is a suggestion made to me by J. P. Pronk and substantiated for Norwegian samples by Soltow [60].

Table 3.XI
Regression coefficients and R found in six cases.[a]

Case	R	Regression coefficient for				Country
		y	z	u	v	
A	0.96	2.95	−0.42	−1.75	.	Netherlands
B	0.94	1.02	−0.33	+0.315	−1.52	United States
C	0.92	0.88	−0.054	+0.083	.	Netherlands (provinces)
D	0.91	−1.04	−0.02	+0.177	.	Netherlands (municipalities)
E	0.89	0.89	+0.27	−0.31	.	Netherlands (provinces)
F	0.86	0.10	+0.27	+0.92	−1.61	Canada (provinces)

[a] Primes used to distinguish variables in Table 3.IV have been omitted in this table.

collect our 'best' cases from the various tables in the order of goodness of fit (Table 3.XI).

There are some regularities in this table worth mentioning. With the exception of case D, which we rejected because of the use of too small geographical units, the coefficients for y (or substitutes) fall from case A to F and so do (even including case D) the negative coefficients for z (or substitutes). Where available the v, representing other factors making for quality, exert considerable influence. This is an argument in favour of introducing such additional variables, as done by Chiswick in an inventive way.

3.5. Cross-section tests, parts of countries, continued

In this section the yardsticks for income inequality and for demand factors will be changed in a further attempt to explore Chiswick's material for the United States. To begin with, the variables used were:

$X' = P(10)$ in Lydall's notation; that is, the upper decile divided by the median of income by state;

$Y' =$ a demand index for third-level educated people, equal to the average ratios of the active population with higher education in the four large sectors (agriculture, manufacturing, trade and transportation, and other services) weighted with the percentages these sectors have among the active population of the state considered;

Z = average years of schooling;

U' = standard deviation (in years of schooling).

The following results were obtained:[*]

$$X' = 0.047 Y' - 0.194Z + 0.160U' + \text{constant}$$
$$(R = 0.77). \tag{3.6}$$

Since $\bar{X}' = 2.28$, and perfect income equality would yield $X' = 1$, halving inequality would require $\Delta X' = -0.64$. This can be obtained, for instance, by halving U', or $\Delta U' = -1.9$, and by changing Z, $\Delta Z = 1.75$, bringing it from 10.2 to 12 years. *Such values seem to be attainable without undue effort.*

Alternatively, using the additional explanatory variable V, income at zero schooling, we obtain

$$X' = 0.029 Y' - 0.112Z + 0.21U' + \text{constant}$$
$$(R = 0.83),$$

from which we infer that income inequality can be halved again by halving U' and, in addition, raising Z from 10.2 to 12.4 years, again without undue effort.

Finally, for the United States three variables were calculated representing excess supply for the three levels of schooling and indicating the difference between supply and demand as calculated before. They are designated T_1, T_2 and T_3, expressed as percentages of the total labour force, and are now used as explanatory variables. The result obtained is

$$X' = 0.0008 T_1 - 0.0326 T_2 - 0.015 T_3 + 2.0$$
$$(R = 0.73), \tag{3.7}$$

Since for the United States as a whole $T_1 + T_2 + T_3 = 0$ and assuming that $\Delta T_3 = 0.3\Delta T_2$, we can estimate the values of the explanatory variables that again would halve X', that is, make $\Delta X' = -0.64$. The resulting values are compared with the observed values for 1960 as follows:

---

[*] F. Wim Blase performed the calculations.

	T_1	T_2	T_3
Observed	12.6	-7.9	-1.1
Required	-9.2	$+8.9$	$+3.9$

In order to judge the degree of realism of the required figures, we have to know the observed values of supply, as percentages of the active population, of the three categories. In 1960, there were around 40 per cent for the first and second level of education and 20 per cent for the third, implying that the changes required do not seem to be out of reach. They do imply the necessity of creating a shortage of people looking for jobs requiring primary education (according to 1960 views) and a surplus of people looking for jobs previously requiring third-level education in order to raise the lowest and to depress the highest incomes.

Another way of judging the feasibility of our new values for T_1, T_2 and T_3 is to analyse the actual 1960 figures for individual states. Thus, while the average for T_1 amounted to 12.6, as already observed, we find seven states where it was ≤ 5; and while the average for T_3 amounted to -1.1, in fourteen states the figure was $\geq +1$.

Our final view on the prospects for income distribution in the United States will be given in Chapter 6, however.

3.6. An incomplete absolute price equation

Finally, a few examples may be presented of an absolute price equation, that is, a price equation for incomes of different groups instead of income distribution parameters. The equations to be presented are incomplete in the sense that they do not include demand factor variables, because either all groups considered are supposed to live under the same demand conditions or no data are available on possibly differing demand conditions for the groups considered.

* I am indebted to Jaap Jansen and Hans Opdam for having performed the computations.

The first and most important example is based on American material taken from Fuchs, which I obtained by the courtesy of Professor Mincer (cf. also [45]).

It supplies us with the average hourly earnings of non-agricultural white males in the USA in 1959, for seven age groups and six groups for the years of completed schooling. We specify that in the following equations x_1 means age, x_2 schooling (both in years), and y earnings in cents per hour. Of course the linearity of the relation is far from certain and we will introduce alternative mathematical expressions. But it appears that already the linear relationship yields a high correlation coefficient; for the complete material we obtain

$$y = 3.48x_1 + 14.5x_2 - 17.2 \qquad (R = 0.88), \qquad (3.8)$$
$$(0.47) \quad\ (1.68)$$

and excluding the highest age group (65 and over) even

$$y = 4.36x_1 + 13.4x_2 - 30.7 \qquad (R = 0.90). \qquad (3.9)$$
$$(0.55) \quad\ (1.69)$$

Figures in parentheses are standard deviations.

A look at the scatter diagram suggests that a curvilinear relationship with respect to both independent variables will significantly improve these results and hence the following two relations were also estimated for the complete material,

$$y = 13.0x_1 + 14.3x_2 - 0.115x_1^2 - 176 \quad (\overline{R} = 0.91),$$
$$(2.55) \quad\ (1.45) \quad\ (0.030) \quad\ (48)$$

$$(3.10)$$

and

$$y = 9.85x_1 - 16.5x_2 + 0.88x_2^2 + 0.35x_1x_2 - 0.120x_1^2 + 15.3$$
$$(1.42) \quad\ (3.6) \quad\ (0.17) \quad\ (0.046) \quad\ (0.017) \quad (32.7)$$

$$(\overline{R} = 0.97). \qquad (3.11)$$

It will be observed that all regression coefficients are significant at the 1 % level, except the intercept. An interesting feature of equation (3.11) is the term x_1x_2 which shows the influence of *'combined scarcities'* of ability and experience.

Table 3.XII

Actual and calculated (in parentheses) values of hourly earnings (cents) of non-agricultural white males with different schooling and age; USA, 1959.

Age	Years of schooling completed					
	2	6.5	10	12	14	17
16	98 (124)	151 (109)	145 (122)	140 (139)	161 (163)	. .
22	148 (160)	171 (154)	177 (174)	190 (196)	209 (224)	226 (280)
29	178 (191)	218 (196)	241 (225)	257 (251)	279 (284)	330 (347)
39	200 (215)	243 (236)	276 (277)	302 (310)	350 (350)	469 (424)
49	195 (215)	254 (252)	278 (305)	316 (345)	403 (392)	533 (476)
59	211 (192)	250 (244)	290 (309)	334 (356)	417 (410)	514 (505)
66	190 (160)	226 (224)	284 (298)	372 (350)	362 (409)	515 (511)

Table 3.XII shows the observed and the estimated values of y for all combinations of x_1 and x_2 (for which the middle values of the intervals have been taken).

The relationship found can also be transformed into one using as independent variables: schooling and work experience $x_3 = x_1 - x_2 - 6$,

$$y = -6.0x_2 + 1.11x_2^2 + 8.4x_3 + 0.11x_2x_3$$
$$- 0.12x_3^2 + 70. \tag{3.12}$$

From (3.12) it appears that increases in x_2, schooling, are paid an increasing income differential, while increases in x_3, experience, are paid a decreasing income differential. Experience is paid a maximum for 30 to 40 years, depending slightly on schooling.

Another, extremely simple, example consists of an estimate based on income and schooling differences between the provinces of the Netherlands. Here a relation was obtained

$$y = 1.37x_2 - 6.3 \qquad (R = 0.92), \tag{3.13}$$
$$(0.09)$$

where y was measured in thousands of guilders (1960) and x_2 in years of schooling completed. The data are those published by the Dutch Central Bureau of Statistics [12].

A number of other studies concerning the impact of personal characteristics on incomes earned have been made by other authors: especially by those belonging to the human capital school, such as Mincer [45] or Chiswick [16]; by authors using samples of individuals, many of whom have been quoted and interpreted by Jencks and his collaborators [33]; and by De Wolff and Van Slijpe [20]. I exclude from this list research on income distribution since most of its results cannot be used directly to get an insight into the question I want to consider as the central issue, namely what is the influence of a number of personal characteristics on income proper (and not on their distribution).

A striking feature of a comparison between the various studies is a considerable difference between inquiries dealing with *groups* of people as their units of observation and inquiries dealing with *individuals* as their units. As a rule much higher correlations are obtained by the former than by the latter. The results given above all show correlation coefficients above 0.9, whereas the results of work with individual data show correlation coefficients of at most 0.7, meaning that at best half of the variance can be explained. This applies to De Wolff and Van Slijpe who, from Husén's [31] material, derive the relationship explaining income with the aid of social class of parents, IQ and years of schooling. Much lower correlations are found, as a rule, by Bowles [5] who arrives at 0.40; in this correlation coefficient a minor contribution is obtained from schooling. Similarly, the correlations found by Chiswick [16] for the states of the USA between the natural logarithm in earnings and years of schooling show a correlation coefficient between 0.33 and 0.57. A possible explanation of this discrepancy is, as mentioned also by Jencks [33], that a number of other factors interfere, such as *non-cognitive skills, demand* factors and just *luck*. The importance of non-cognitive skills may be illustrated by an attempt to explain income differences in the Netherlands by differences in degree of independence. These, even though measured in a very crude way, alone show an $r = 0.89$, again for 21 groups (Chapter 4, Table 4.II).

Because of my adherence to a demand–supply theory I also submit that in addition to personal characteristics demand factors co-determine an individual's income. The neglected supply (non-cognitive) and demand factors evidently do not correlate strongly with schooling; otherwise the correlation coefficients for inquiries with individuals would have been higher. But they must cancel each other out a good deal, otherwise the group correlations with schooling would not be so high. This latter assumption may be tested by comparing the values of the regression coefficients found in some inquiries with groups with the values found from inquiries with individuals.

The influence of one more year of schooling on incomes expressed in dollars per year can be derived from the linear equations (3.8) and (3.9) by multiplying the influence on hourly earnings by the number of working hours per year divided by 100, amounting roughly to 20. The results are 268 to 290 if we take the regression coefficients of x_2, and 356 to 360 if we replace x_1 by the expression $x_1 = x_3 + x_2 + 6$, x_3 representing years of work experience.

From the results obtained by De Wolff and Van Slijpe, using the coefficients in front of Z_4 (which the authors report to be the most important) in equations 16 and 18, respectively, we find for one more year of schooling an income difference of 1700 respectively 1400 Swedish kronor, or about $ 340 and $ 280.

From the analysis using the provinces of the Netherlands, equation (3.13), we find Dfl. 1370 or $ 380.

While it is significant, on the one hand, that the orders of magnitude are the same, it is also significant that the American figures are lower than the Dutch figure. Keeping in mind that the Swedish figures refer to people of age 35, we find that the corresponding figure for the USA is lower than the Swedish figure too. This reflects a lower scarcity of more qualified people in the USA than in Sweden and than in the Netherlands.

Chiswick [16] finds that this same difference is shown by the negative correlation (-0.79) between (1) the regression coefficients of ln E (natural logarithm of earnings) on years of schooling and (2) the states' income (averages of natural logarithms [16] Table 3-3). In addition the regression coefficient is higher (0.14) for Puerto Rico than for the USA (0.11), [16] Table 4-2. Support for the thesis that income differences between groups with different schooling correlate inversely with their scarcity can also be found in historical comparisons as made for the period 1900–1963 in the USA by Ullman [74] Table 3.

So far we have assumed that relative scarcity is mainly changed by changes in supply. Historically these changes have been considerable and over a long period such as the one considered by Ullman [74], 1900–1963, they are largely responsible for the reduction in income inequality. There are also changes in demand, however, which affect relative scarcity. In Chapter 6, I have tried to disentangle these two influences and found that in fact it is a 'race' between supply (by education) and demand (by technological development) which determines the changes in relative scarcity of any type of manpower.

In conclusion we may state that for large groups of individuals with different schooling and different length of work experience their income averages differ significantly. Correlations obtained for such group characteristics and their incomes are above 0.9 in the cases analysed statistically, covering the United States (1959) and the Netherlands (1960). The lower correlations found in inquiries with individuals need not be ascribed to random factors or 'luck' only; there are other personal characteristics which affect incomes, such as independence, health and family size. In addition, demand factors play a role; and relative scarcity is the more important explanation of income differences.

This implies that the income increase to be obtained by one more year of education can be read from our formulae for only small numbers of persons who make a decision of whether or not to increase schooling. The additional income obtainable is not a fixed amount for all countries or all times; we found it to be higher, the lower the average income of the countries considered.

Among the inquiries made with single persons, there remains, for the time being, an as yet unsolved contrast between, for instance, Bowles who finds a very limited influence of schooling and results obtained by De Wolff and Van Slijpe and the present author who find a significant influence. These are not necessarily due to the choice of the other explanatory variables used in the regression equations.

4

Supply factors and utility or welfare

4.1. Utility function as the source of supply

Economists agree that an individual's supply behaviour concerning production factors and in particular labour derives from the maximization of his utility function under the restrictions prevailing. These restrictions are usually supposed to consist of the prices prevailing in the market compartments to which the individual has access and the individual's own characteristics. Agreement among economists stops when the question is asked whether the utility function can be specified by quantitative observations or *measurement*. The overwhelming majority of the profession denies this possibility. Cassel for this reason preferred not to use utility functions at all and to base economic science on supply (and demand) functions without an attempt to give them a deeper foundation. Here lies a danger of inconsistencies, however; and most economists prefer to maintain the concept of utility, adding, though, that only supply behaviour can be measured. Although the measurements so far presented in this study are not affected by the controversy on the measurability of utility and although the question of how income distribution can be influenced, can be dealt with without making use of such measurement, we will choose in favour of a quantitative specification of utility or welfare. One reason is the avoidance, already mentioned, of inconsistencies; another the gain of clarity obtained in the search for additional supply factors, one of the obvious lacunae in this field of research. A final reason for our choice is the necessity of a specification if we want to give content to the notions of an *optimal* and of an *equitable* income distribution – two different concepts, both of considerable practical importance. I want to add that my choice in favour of measurement of utility or welfare is shared, although with a different elaboration, by Van Praag and his collaborators [79, 80].

4.2. Specification of utility function

In order to avoid misunderstanding I want to state from the outset that I am not claiming that the treatment to be proposed and to be tried out in a first few steps is part of economic science only. It contains elements which may be named, respectively, (i) *methodological* or *philosophical* and (ii) *ethical* or *moralist*. What matters of course is not so much whether a contribution to the solution of a problem belongs to the realm of one or of another science or discipline; rather it is whether indeed a contribution is made.

To start with I submit [65] that three elements enter into a utility or welfare function, to be called variables, parameters and constants or coefficients. *Variables* are elements changing over time and among individuals. Some of them can be chosen by the individual (or the household) considered, others cannot. The most important choice variable in our context is the choice of a *job* or *occupation*. Examples of variables not under his control are changes in wage or salary scale or the general price level, in brief the socio-economic environment. This statement reflects my opinion that man-made monopolies are less important than is sometimes believed. The theory can be adapted to a different belief, however. Whereas in our context the choice of one's job is the most important one, for young generations the choice of *education* is the central one, not unrelated, of course, to an implied choice of occupation. Jobs can be represented by figures such as are supplied by *job evaluation;* or, alternatively, occupations can be represented by their occupational status [33].

Parameters are supposed to be constants for the individuals (or households) in the time span considered, but to vary among them. They characterize the individuals, households, or even groups of these under consideration. There are two groups of parameters: those characterizing the *productive capabilities* and those characterizing the *consumption needs*. Among the former, cognitive capabilities as shown by IQ stand out, but are by no means the only ones. Other features, corresponding for instance to the aspects used in job evaluation, are important too. We may think of the capacity to decide and act independently, as required for leading positions; of the willingness to co-operate with others; persistence, technical intuition, and so on and so forth. For lack of information we may sometimes replace a real parameter by a dummy. In our first step of applying the theory we will take as an important productive parameter *years of schooling* completed, which in actual fact is not exactly a parameter, but probably approximately so. Psychologists such as Duncan [23] and Jencks [33] have dug deeper already and eventually their work should be integrated into ours.

Of the second group of parameters, those reflecting needs, we think of *family size* as an important dummy; even though for certain problems again, it is essential to go back to its determinants. If in coming periods birth control is to play an important role, we must be aware of the desire to have at least a few children as a very important component of happiness. In the context of a poor population without an old-age pension children are a form of social insurance – and so on. Another group of need parameters is based on the individual's *health* and may therefore be represented by some health indicator. For larger groups of households these parameters may not in the average vary much and may therefore be disregarded. Inquiries based on individual households cannot neglect them.

Coming to the *coefficients*, these are the intensities by which variables and parameters affect utility or welfare; and here our methodological approach is that they are considered the same for all individuals/households considered. As soon as some student of welfare maintains that such an intensity is not equal for all, he is talking about a parameter, not a coefficient. The set of coefficients should be seen as characterizing the human species or some subspecies, in contradistinction to other animals. They may also be considered as an expression of some sort of *'equivalence'* of all human beings, dealt with in more depth in Chapter 8.

Mathematically the coefficients also depend on the functional shape given to the utility or welfare function and here we have, as is well known, some degrees of freedom. We have a choice between all functions which can be obtained from each other by monotonous transformations and we are free to choose some appropriate form as long as observations do not refute it. A simple example chosen to be used in this book is

$$\omega_i = \ln \{ x_i - c_0 s_i - \tfrac{1}{2} c_2 (s_i - v_i)^2 \}, \tag{4.1}$$

where

ω_i is household i's utility,

x_i income after tax in thousands of guilders per annum,

s_i represents the job held by the head of the household, expressed in required level of schooling (in units of three years),

v_i actually attained level of schooling in the same units,

c_0 and c_2 coefficients.

This choice is extremely simple, as a first step to illustrate our procedure. It contains two variables, namely x_i and s_i, and one parameter v_i. It may be interpreted as a function of *consumable income corrected for two inconveniences*, namely the effort required* by the job $c_0 s_i$ (or, if c_0 were found to be negative, the additional satisfaction, on top of that of income, experienced in the job), and the inconvenience (or *tension*) experienced by a possible divergency between required and actual schooling. This tension is supposed to be equal for positive and negative divergencies of the same size. Since generally the tension will not be large, the quadratic function

---

* There is empirical evidence that working hours differ little for fully-employed persons in a large spectrum of jobs; hence no attempt was made to introduce this variable.

is a sufficient approximation in the neighbourhood of the minimum tension. An alternative function will be discussed in Section 4.6.

No other term in v_i has been included. There are two ways of interpreting this further simplification. One is that the only way in which a higher capability v_i affects welfare is that the level of reference for the *tension* is shifted, but that the only thing that matters for the tension is the divergence in years between required and actual schooling. The other interpretation is that we *cannot know* an additional (say, linear) term in v_i, since by definition nobody can shift from one value of it to another. If we supplement this ignorance with the assumption that a higher level of capability affects welfare positively, leaving out the term in v_i means that we underestimate welfare more the higher v_i is and that our estimates of welfare differences are underestimations. As we shall see, this strengthens our main conclusion about the inequity of the present income distribution (Chapters 7 and 8).

4.3. Two methods of measuring welfare

So far in the Netherlands two methods of estimating the welfare of various individual households or groups of households have been tried out. These two methods have been used alternatively for many other purposes as well. The first is to *interview* the (heads of) households themselves. This method has been used by Van Praag and collaborators [79, 80], who interviewed 3000 members of the Belgian and 3000 members of the Dutch consumer union. The second method consists of observing people's *behaviour* rather than their stated opinions. The advantage of the first method is that a set of figures is obtained, based on a uniform set of questions and also containing figures for individuals with unequal capabilities; a disadvantage is that experience in other cases has shown that opinions do not always correspond with later behaviour. Somebody earning Dfl. 15,000 at the moment of the interview in Van Praag's inquiries does not only state what level of satisfaction he feels with this actual income, but also states the level he would experience with an income of Dfl. 20,000. If he later actually earns the latter amount, will he maintain his statement? The material collected already suggests he will not ('preference drift' is observed). The advantage of the second method is that only behaviour is observed, but the disadvantage is that this excludes comparison between households whose heads show differing capabilities, as already observed. This isn't true if one accepts our argument to include no other term with v_i.

It goes without saying that Van Praag and I are working on an attempt to use his material in order to cross-check my findings. The results, which at the moment of writing, are not yet available in final form, will be published elsewhere. In this book the results of the second method only will be dealt with.

4.4. A test based on material for the Netherlands, 1962

The main test made of the utility function (4.1) was based on statistical material for the Netherlands in 1962.

(a) The essential characteristic of the material is its subdivision of the labour market into 21 compartments, later reduced to 19, each compartment being characterized by its s and v, where s is assumed to be the upper quartile of the corresponding v-distribution. The statistical material used is shown in Table 4.I and the way it has been estimated is described in the Annex. Since v is supposed to reflect the (only) parameter in the utility function and free competition is assumed to exist, a free choice of all individuals with a given v_i between the compartments showing that v is possible; and the coexistence of various values of s in these compartments enables us to test the relation, derived from (4.1),

$$x_i - c_0 s_i - c_1 v_i - \tfrac{1}{2}c_2(s_i - v_i)^2$$
$$= x_j - c_0 s_j - c_1 v_i - \tfrac{1}{2}c_2(s_j - v_i)^2. \qquad (4.2)$$

Some terms in v_i cancel each other out. We can use as observation pairs any two pairs with equal v_i for all values of i.

Table 4.I

Estimated income distribution of the Netherlands, 1962, according to schooling (v), required schooling (s) and degree of independence (W, alternatively W').

s		v 2	3	4	5	6	W (W')	Description of main groups included
6	f			0.1	0.3	0.9		Free professions;
	l			42.3	42.3	42.3	2	Directors of limited
	l'			19.0	19.0	19.0	(6)	companies
	x			14.0	14.0	14.0		
5	f		1.5	1.1	0.5	0.7		Independent industrialists;
	l		19.5	19.5	19.5	19.5	1	Teaching staff of secon-
	l'		14.2	14.2	14.2	14.2	(5)	dary and third level
	x		11.3	11.3	11.3	11.3		
4	f	0.7	5.3	4.4	1.3	0.1		Civil servants in general
	l	10.2	10.2	10.2	10.2	10.2	0	service; Private employees
	l'	9.7	9.7	9.7	9.7	9.7	(2)	
	x	8.3	8.3	8.3	8.3	8.3		
3	f	0.1	4.0	1.0	0.1			Independents in trade
	l	15.0	16.2	17.4	18.6		1	and services
	l'	12.0	12.5	13.0	13.4		(3)	
	x	9.9	10.2	10.5	10.8			
2	f	10.7	6.6	0.1				Primary school teachers;
	l	8.9	10.8	12.7			0	Part of administrative
	l'	8.5	10.2	11.3			(2)	personnel; Police; Mining
	x	7.4	9.0	9.4				workers; Farmers
2	f	46.6	13.8					Workers, incl. Retail trade
	l	5.3	8.4				0	employees; Part of
	l'	4.9	8.1				(2)	administrative personnel
	x	4.4	7.1					

Symbol definition :

f : Frequency in per cent of number of taxpayers.

l : Income in thousands of guilders.

l' : Labour income contained in l.

x : Labour income after tax.

The correlations found are unsatisfactory, however, cf. Table 4.II, cases A–E. As a consequence, the theory in its initial form *had to be rejected*. The correlation coefficient between $x_i - x_j$ and $z_{ij} = (s_i - v_i)^2 - (s_j - v_i)^2$ indicated by x and z in Table 4.II, is low (0.14) and the regression coefficients, even after the introduction of other explanatory variables, are insignificant. A new variable which seemed to have high explanatory power will now be discussed.

(b) The description of the social groups under consideration suggested that an additional capability is relevant, namely the ability to make independent decisions. The groups considered were divided into three groups with decisions of increasing importance; the groups are represented by a parameter W. Persons having to make decisions of minor importance only and usually described as socially dependent were given the value $W = 0$; persons heading small and medium-sized enterprises, $W = 1$; and heads of limited companies or persons in liberal professions, $W = 2$. As can be seen from cases A–E in Table 4.II, satisfactory correlations were only obtained when W was included. This state of affairs constitutes a classic example of the necessity of introducing an additional element into a theory in order to fit the facts in a more satisfactory way. The basic idea may also be expressed as the capability of giving guidance to other people, a capability given a central place in income distribution by Tuck [73]. An alternative scale W' was chosen and is also shown in Table 4.I.

(c) The *interpretation* of the role of W poses some questions, however. Must we consider W as a parameter, as suggested, which implies that it indicates an innate personal capability; or must we consider it as a job variable? I opted for the first interpretation, which gives to W a role comparable to the role of v in the simplest model. This implies that we have to consider as separate groups not only those having a different v, but also those having a different set of v and W; Table 4.III indicates the arrangement of our statistical material corresponding to that interpretation. This arrangement reduces the number of observations to six pairs (each with another set v, W).

It appears that significant results can now be obtained (Table 4.II, cases F, G and H). They differ because in case F the

Table 4.II
Results of testing the two theories by equating utility between cells with same v (Theory I, cases A through E) or between cells with same v and W (cases F, G, H).

Case no.	N	Regression coefficients for x on							Simple corr. between x and				Const. term e	Mult. corr. coeff.
		z	w	q	q'	q''	m	v	z	w	q	v		
A	16	0.16 (0.13)	1.58 (0.63)	−0.20 (0.20)	–	–	–	–	0.14	0.89	−0.83	–	+0.57	0.91
B	16	0.17 (0.14)	–	−0.10 (0.37)	–	–	–	–	0.14	0.89	−0.83	–	+0.49	0.88
C	16	0.16 (0.13)	1.61 (0.96)	−0.21 (0.35)	–	–	−0.01 (0.37)	–	0.14	0.89	−0.83	–	+0.57	0.91
D	12	0.10 (0.21)	–	–	−0.01 (0.21)	0.17 (0.08)	–	–	0.14	0.89	−0.83	–	+0.19 (0.45)	0.80
E	16	0.15 (0.13)	2.13 (0.29)	–	–	–	–	–	0.14	0.89	−0.83	–	+0.55 (0.27)	0.90
F[a]	6	0.44 (0.12)	–	–	–	–	–	1.10 (0.40)	0.63	–	–	−0.20	−3.6 (1.42)	0.91
G[b]	6	0.28 (0.28)	–	–	–	–	–	−0.17 (0.44)	0.79	–	–	−0.70	+1.47 (3.34)	0.79
H[b]	6	0.32 (0.10)	–	–	–	–	–	–	0.79	–	–	–	+0.9 (0.5)	0.79

[a] The lowest row of observations in Table 4.I has been excluded.
[b] The lowest two rows of observations in Table 4.I have been combined.

Symbol definition:

m : wv.

w : $W_1 - W_2$.

N : Number of observations of differences between two cells with same utility.

x : Differences in labour income after tax between two cells or $x_1 - x_2$.

z : $s_1^2 - s_2^2 - 2 v(s_1 - s_2)$; s schooling required, v schooling available.

q : $W_1^2 - W_2^2 - v(W_1 - W_2)$, W degree of independence (as in Table 4.I).

q' : $W_1'^2 - W_2'^2 - v(W_1' - W_2')$, W' degree of independence (same, but 5 levels instead of 3).

q'' : $W_1''^2 - W_2''^2$.

lowest line of Table 4.I has not been used, since the category
for $v = 2$ contains a group of holiday workers which somewhat
depresses the income figure. Since, however, the figure covers
also a large portion of ordinary workers, it was decided to
include them, by combining them with the other group with
$s = 2$. This yielded cases G and H. Since in case G, in addition,
the influence of v became insignificant, case H was added. This
provided us with some further insight into the sensitivity of e,
representing the influence of s on x and hence on ω. While in
case F (valid for the half of the population with high incomes)
the influence of s was found to be negative, in case H (valid for
the population as a whole) this influence was found to be
positive. These findings are interesting since their meaning is
that for higher incomes the attractiveness of a higher s job
surpasses its disutility, while for lower incomes the opposite
applies. Notwithstanding its lower multiple correlation coefficient we take case H as the most satisfactory result because (i)
its coefficients take an intermediate place between those of
cases F and G and (ii) because its coefficients are theoretically
more attractive, while (iii) it will keep us, because of the sign
of the constant term, on the safe side in our estimation of the
optimal and the just income distribution. Written in the form
of (4.2) the relationship runs:

$$x_1 - 0.45s_1 - \tfrac{1}{2} \cdot 0.64(s_1 - v_j)^2$$
$$= x_2 - 0.45s_2 - \tfrac{1}{2} \cdot 0.64(s_2 - v_j)^2, \qquad (4.3)$$

where

$s_1 = 2, 2, 3, 2, 3, 3;$
$s_2 = s_1 + 2;$
$v_j = 2, 3, 3, 4, 4, 5.$
   This corresponds with

$$\omega = \ln \left\{ x - 0.45s - 0.32(s - v)^2 \right\} \qquad (4.4)$$

as the resulting utility or welfare function.
   (d) Whether W is a parameter or a variable, in both cases
we must face the problem of what the corresponding variable

Table 4.III
Distribution of labour income after tax over values of s, v and W (degree of independence).

v	2		3		4			5			6		
s / W	0	1	0	1	0	1	2	0	1	2	0	1	2
6							14.0			14.0			14.0
5				11.3		11.3			11.3			11.3	
4	8.3		8.3		8.3			8.3			8.3		
3		9.9		10.2		10.5			10.8				
2	7.4		9.0		9.4								
2	4.4		7.1										

or parameter must be to define the 'tension' concept introduced in Section 4(b). For lack of observations the only alternative I investigated assumes that in the case where W is considered a job variable rather than a personal parameter, the corresponding parameter is again v. This requires the introduction of an expression $(W - \beta v)^2$ instead of W as an explanatory variable, where β is a scale coefficient to be estimated from regression analysis. The results of this attempt will be found in Table 4.II, cases A–E, from which it becomes clear that:

(i) correlations were substantially improved $(R \gg r_{xz})$ by the introduction of $W_1 - W_2$ or w, as shown even in $r_{xw} = 0.89$, and

(ii) attempts to introduce $(W - \beta v)^2$ were unsuccessful; they did not improve the multiple correlation and the expression $(W - \beta v)^2$ obtained insignificant regression coefficients; from this I conclude that W is a personal parameter rather than a job variable to be approached by schooling.

(e) As long as in fact parameters v or W are innate, incomes will depend on them as a consequence of a relative *scarcity* of these human properties. Comparisons of the type of (4.2) using different values of v (or W) instead of s and the same values of s on both sides will not reflect the psychological impact on ω of v (or W), but its relative scarcity, that is, the impact of the difference between demand for and supply of the capability considered. Since the frontier between scarcity and power is difficult to draw, one may even interpret the additional scarcity income received by those endowed with a high value of v or W as an income derived from 'power' and see it as an element of 'exploitation'.*

4.5. A test based on material for Illinois

The basic tool of the simplest test shown in the previous section is a two-entry table showing incomes of individuals arranged according to education (horizontal) and occupation (vertical), both measured in comparable units. In the primitive stage of the testing shown vertical differences are the object of free choice, whereas horizontal differences are scarcity differences due to the impossibility of shifting horizontally. For lack of more information and by way of experiment, census data for Illinois were used with the heroic assumption that the main non-farm occupational groups (h) placed in the order of their average incomes, require the education, in terms of school years completed, indicated in the left-hand column of Table 4.IV.

The sum of the totals of the occupational groups given by Dougherty [22] falls short by 441 (thousand persons) of the sum of the totals of the educational groups. In order to arrive at an identical grand total these 441 without occupation were distributed proportionally over the occupation classes.

Thus, the column and row indicated 'total' in Table 4.IV were given. In order to fill in the cells of the table the method of the northwest-corner rule was applied, well known from the 'Hitchcock problem' [30, 43]. The method may be interpreted as an 'optimum' use of the available manpower in the various occupation classes. Here optimum means the *cheapest way of having the jobs done*, in the sense of using people with the lowest education available first and only adding people with higher education as long as not sufficient cheaper manpower

---

* Interesting enough, a case of 'exploitation' by *human* capital.

Table 4.IV
Estimated employment according education *h'* and occupation *h*; Illinois, 1959, in thousands of male equivalents.

h				*h'*					Total	Denomination
	0	3	6	8	10	12	14	18		
0	54	155	.	.	.	.	.	.	209	Labourers
3	.	12	287	.	.	.	.	.	299	Service workers
6	.	.	127	638	.	.	.	.	765	Operatives
8	.	.	.	90	455	.	.	.	545	Clerical workers
10	.	.	.	.	198	439	.	.	637	Craftsmen
12	.	.	.	.	.	233	.	.	233	Sales workers
14	.	.	.	.	.	88	286	.	374	Professionals, technicians
18	.	.	.	.	.	.	15	304	319	Administrators, proprietors
Total	54	167	414	728	653	760	301	304	3381	

was available. As could be expected, only a number of cells around the main diagonal are non-empty, but enough of them to make vertical comparisons possible, that is comparisons of groups with the same education but in different occupations.

The next step is to estimate the incomes for the non-empty cells. As income we take the average of the column and of the row average income. Thus, for cell (1; 1) we take the average of 2.8 and 3.9, rounded to 3.4; and so on. This produces Table 4.V. In the 'average' column and row the cell figures have been averaged, using as weights the employment figures of Table 4.IV. In brackets the true averages have been added and it will be seen that the deviations between our 'estimated' and the observed average incomes are not large.

The units chosen for *h'* are, as already said, years of schooling; in order to attain a crude degree of commensurability between *h* and *h'* the eight occupation classes have been numbered in the same way, suggesting that these figures

Table 4.V
Average earnings for the cells of Table 4.IV, estimated as the averages of the column and the row average average observed and placed in parentheses; Illinois, 1959, in thousands of US $.

h	h'								Average
	0	3	6	8	10	12	14	18	
0	3.4	3.6							3.5 (3.9)
3		3.7	4.1						4.1 (4.0)
6			4.6	5.1					5.0 (5.1)
8				5.1	5.7				5.6 (5.2)
10					6.4	6.9			6.7 (6.6)
12						7.5			7.5 (7.8)
14						8.2	9.0		8.7 (9.3)
18							9.7	11.1	11.0 (10.8)
Average	3.4	3.6	4.2	5.1	5.9	7.2	9.0	11.1	
	(2.8)	(3.3)	(4.2)	(5.0)	(6.2)	(7.1)	(8.6)	(11.3)	

represent the education required for each of the occupation classes.

Since income after tax appears in our welfare function, Table 4.VI has been calculated from Table 4.V by the deduction of personal income taxes as prevailing in 1959.

As announced, the estimation of coefficients c_0 and c_2 will be based on the comparison of vertical variations in Table 4.VI, since these refer to groups with the same parameter h'. We exclude from the eight cases involved the lower element in column $h' = 12$, since the $h = 12$ and $h = 14$ professions not only differ in h value, but also in the degree of independence needed for the two groups of professions; this leaves us with seven cases. We followed a similar procedure for the Netherlands in Section 4.4.

For each pair of observations we assume that their welfare figures are equal since free mobility between the two is possible; hence,

$$x_1 - c_0 h_1 - \tfrac{1}{2}c_2(h_1 - h')^2$$
$$= x_2 - c_0 h_2 - \tfrac{1}{2}c_2(h_2 - h')^2, \qquad (4.5)$$

Table 4.VI
Incomes after personal income tax for the cells shown in Tables 4.IV and 4.V.

h	h'						
	0	3	6	8	10	12	14	18
0	3.1	3.3						
3		3.4	3.7					
6			4.2	4.6				
8				4.6	5.1			
10					5.7	6.2		
12						6.7		
14						7.2	7.8	
18							8.4	9.5

where suffix 1 refers to the lower and suffix 2 to the higher h in the pair.

Equation (4.5) reduces to

$$x_1 - x_2 \tag{4.6}$$
$$= c_0(h_1 - h_2) + \tfrac{1}{2}c_2\{h_1^2 - h_2^2 - 2h'(h_1 - h_2)\}.$$

Replacing the left-hand side by x, the expression in parentheses on the right-hand side by h and the expression in brackets by z, (4.6) reduces to

$$x = c_0 h + \tfrac{1}{2}c_2 z. \tag{4.7}$$

For six pairs of observations contained in Table 4.VI this equation can be tested, assuming that no constant term appears on the right-hand side. Writing $\bar{x}$ for the average and x' for $x - \bar{x}$, and similarly for h and z, the assumption can be written

$$\bar{x} - \gamma_0 \bar{h} - \tfrac{1}{2}\gamma_2 \bar{z} = 0, \tag{4.8}$$

where γ_0 and γ_2 are the estimates of c_0 and c_2. Assumption (4.8) links γ_0 and γ_2 and reduces our regression to a single regression because

$$\gamma_2 = -0.33 + 2.29\gamma_0. \tag{4.9}$$

The dependent variable is $X = x' + 0.164z'$ and the independent one is $H = h' + 1.14z'$, for the first regression. For it we find

$$X = 0.144H \qquad (R = 0.98), \qquad (4.10)$$

and for the second regression,

$$X = 0.149H.$$

Transformed back into the original variables we find, for the two regressions,

$$x = 0.144h + 0.00z,$$

respectively,

$$x = 0.149h + 0.007z, \qquad (4.11)$$

meaning that in Frisch's [26] bunch-map-analysis way $c_0 = 0.146 \pm 0.003$ and $c_2 = 0.07 \pm 0.07$.

The utility function for Illinois thus becomes

$$\omega = \ln \{x - 0.146h - 0.03(h - h')^2\}. \qquad (4.12)$$

For a comparison with the Dutch utility function (4.4) we have to transform the latter, where x is expressed in guilders (the buying power of which was roughly that of \$ 0.5) and schooling s or v in units of 3 years. Expressed in \$, h and h', the Dutch utility function then becomes

$$\omega_{NL} = \ln 2 + \ln \{x - 0.075h - 0.018(h - h')^2\}.$$

$$(4.13)$$

This means that the disutility of work requiring one more year of education is half as large for the average Dutchman as for the man from Illinois and the disutility of the 'tension' one-third as large.

4.6. Test results for some other American states

In a future publication some alternative tests of the measurement of utility functions for seven American states, including Illinois, will be discussed in detail. Some provisional results may be given here, in order to widen the background of our first attempts, given in this chapter. As a consequence of the results obtained with the material for six additional states, the method described in Section 4.5 has been supplemented with a second method, to be called the *linear*, as distinct from the *quadratic tension method* shown in that section. The words quadratic and linear refer to the 'tension term', specified as $\frac{1}{2}c_2(h - h')^2$ in Section 4.5 and alternatively as $\frac{1}{2}c_2' |h - h'|$, where the tension between education required, h, and actual education completed, h', is measured by the absolute value of their difference $z' = |h - h'|$ instead of by the squared difference. One reason why this second method was applied was that the results show a high degree of sensitivity of the main coefficient c_0 to this choice. Another reason was that the quadratic tension method sometimes yielded c_2 values with the wrong sign. This was also the case with the linear tension method, however. A further complication of the linear method is the identity of Δh [cf. equation (4.7)] and $\Delta z'$, preventing the identification of c_0 and c_2'. This complication was removed by assuming the value of $\frac{1}{2}c_2'$ to be equal, for all states, to the value found for Wisconsin, which is the smaller of the two values with the correct sign obtained. Since this value is small and two of the states yielded $c_2' < 0$, a third theory, the '*simple linear theory*', was also applied, where $c_2' = 0$. In all cases the restriction (4.8) had to be obeyed.

The main findings have been summarized in Table 4.VII. Some of these findings are:

(i) Correlations between X and H appearing in equation (4.10) are very satisfactory for three more states, but much less so for New York and Michigan. For New York the heterogeneity of the labour force may be an explanation. Because of these lower correlation coefficients R it is of some importance to distinguish between diagonal and first regression coefficients; theoretically the latter are more relevant, since we can take it for granted that our equations omit some significant additional independent variables.

(ii) The values obtained for c_0 applying the linear or no

Table 4.VII

Values of c_0, $\frac{1}{2}c_2$ and R found for seven American states using three methods:: (i) quadratic tension, (ii) linear tension, (iii) no tension ('simply theory').

| State | Value of c_0 using | | | | | | Value of $\frac{1}{2}c_2$ using | |
| | (i) | | | (ii) | | (iii) | (i) | (ii) |
	Diag. regr.	1st regr.	R	c_0	R			
Cal	0.283	0.244	0.86	0.120	0.74	0.113	0.052	*
Ill	0.146	0.144	0.98	0.148	0.39	0.144	0.006	0.019
NY	0.350	0.250	0.71	0.124	0.43	0.116	0.083	*
Mich	0.227	0.171	0.75	0.111	0.71	0.103	0.038	*
SoCa	0.092	0.091	1.00	0.096	0.58	0.091	−0.004	−0.015
Tex	0.108	0.107	0.98	0.116	0.40	0.113	−0.005	−0.026
Wis	0.108	0.106	0.98	0.098	0.98	0.094	0.008	0.0077

Note : Asterisk means cases where $\Delta h = \Delta z'$ for all observations and c_2 is indeterminate.

tension version are considerably more uniform and closer to the values found for the Netherlands in equation (4.13).

(iii) The correlation coefficients found for the linear tension method are much lower. A closer look at the figures shows that some of the higher R for the quadratic theory are due, however, to the common term in z' of X and H, which becomes preponderant for some states. Anyway the R's are correlation coefficients between income differences and differences in h and much lower than the correlation between incomes and h.

4.7. Appendix on estimation of figures of Table 4.I

These figures have been estimated mainly with the aid of (i) the Netherlands Census of Population of 1960 which gives information on the school achievements of a number of two-digit social groups; (ii) tax statistics for 1964 giving incomes before and after tax for a smaller number (21) of socio-economic groups, and (iii) income distribution statistics for 1966 where labour income and income from other sources are shown. The exact names of the three sources are: (i) 13e Algemene Volkstelling, Deel 8 (13th General Census, Part 8) p. 62, 72 ff.; (ii) Nota over de Inkomensverdeling, Bijlage 15, Miljoenennota 1970 (Memorandum on Income Distribution, Annex 15, Budget Proposals 1970) p. 15; (iii) Inkomensverdeling 1966 en Vermogensverdeling 1967 (Income Distribution 1966 and Distribution of Wealth 1967) pp. 80–83.

Sources (i) and (iii) are publications of the Netherlands Central Bureau of Statistics; source (ii) is a parliamentary document. All can be obtained from the Staatsuitgeverij (Government Stationery Office), The Hague.

Since source (ii) refers to a smaller number of social groups than source (i), the latter's groups have been combined so as to cover the larger groups of (ii); even these have not been kept separate, however, but have been combined if they showed almost equal incomes and almost equal social status (especially comparable degrees of independence). As already observed in the main text, v is the actual amount of schooling completed,

Table 4.VIII
Comparison of US median and Dutch upper quartile schooling.

US groups		NL groups		US median (18–64 years old)	NL upper quartile
No.	Brief description	No.	Brief description		
A	Professionals, technicians, etc.	0	Professionals, specialists	16.3	15
B/I	Farmers and farm workers	4	Agrarian occupations, fishing	8.3	9
C	Managers, officers, proprietors	1	Managers, high officers	12.5	12
D	Clerical and kindred workers	2	Administrative occupations	12.4	9
E	Sales workers	3	Commercial occupations	12.5	9
F/G	Craftsmen, foremen, operators	7/8	Handicraft and industry	10.2	9
H	Service workers	6/9	Services	10.0	9
J	Labourers excl. farmers, miners	5	Mining, peat digging	8.7	6

as measured in periods of 3 years, and s the corresponding upper quartile. For approximately ten one-digit social groups, s has been compared with the median of school years (in units of 1 year) completed by the American active population between 18 and 64 years (US Department of Commerce, Current Population Reports, Series P 20, No. 207, p. 27; and US Census of Population 1960, Educational Attainment, Final Report PC (2) – 5B, p. 136). There was no systematic deviation, apart from a few years average difference. The comparison is crude anyway because the Dutch figures are expressed in multiples of three years only; the number of years of schooling is not given in the publications, but only the frequency distribution over five main school types. The reader should again be reminded of the illustrative character of the entire econometric material offered in this chapter. The figures for the large social groups are given in Table 4.VIII.

5

Demand factors and the production function

5.1. Production function as a source of demand

Demand for production factors is exerted by the organizers of production. These organizers of production may either be private entrepreneurs or managers of publicly owned plants. They combine quantities of the various production factors in order to obtain certain quantities of product. Whatever the criterion guiding the organizers – maximum profit or the satisfaction of a given demand at given prices – they have to know what product they can obtain with the aid of given quantities of production factors. Depending on the prices at which they can attract the production factors needed they will combine the latter in different proportions.

For quite some time the production factors considered in macro-economic production functions were *land*, *labour* and *capital* only; and, to begin with, only their quantities were considered. Since for the economy as a whole the quantity of land can be considered constant, land has often been left out altogether. A first improvement made consisted of the introduction of technical development as an additional factor which increases exponentially over time. As a further improvement *technological development* was expressed as quality changes in capital or in labour or in both. In order to study income distribution, especially between various types of labour, we have to introduce these *types of labour* separately into a macro-economic production function. Recently this has been undertaken by a number of authors, in particular by Bowles [5], Dougherty [22], Kuipers [37] and Ullman [74]. In this study a slightly different approach will be followed, but we shall on occasion compare it with the approaches of the authors mentioned. Since for the time being the best data available and relevant to our problem are those about schooling, we will restrict ourselves to this characteristic. But even if we stick to the use of only one aspect of the quality of labour, namely the quantity of schooling, we must make a difference between the schooling normally *required* for the execution of a given productive task and the *actual* schooling of the person engaged for that task. In this simple first approach only three levels of education will be considered, namely, the first, the second and the third level, as usually distinguished. The quantities of persons engaged will be expressed by a symbol ϕ_{sv}, where ϕ is the portion of the total active population carrying out tasks for which preferably the level s (1, 2 or 3) is required but for which people with level v are being used. Knowing that they will not always succeed in attracting people with $v = s$, the organizers of production will also try to obtain people with $v \neq s$ and they are supposed to know what the contribution to production of such people will be; this is expressed in the production function. In a situation where fewer people of highest schooling are available than could be used in the production process a rational behaviour of both the demand and the supply side of the market will imply that $v \leq s$. The total active population can be represented by the matrix of Table 5.I.

Table 5.I

Matrix of active population, assuming (a) full employment, (b) scarcity of educated manpower and (c) three levels of education.

Schooling required	Actual schooling v			Total
s	1	2	3	
1	ϕ_{11}	.	.	$\phi_{1.}$
2	ϕ_{21}	ϕ_{22}	.	$\phi_{2.}$
3	.	ϕ_{32}	ϕ_{33}	$\phi_{3.}$
Total	$\phi_{.1}$	$\phi_{.2}$	$\phi_{.3}$	1

Although it is conceivable that $\phi_{31} \neq 0$, it is not rational and the actual figure is small enough to be neglected. This means that, apart from capital and land, we have five production factors in the realm of labour.

A more general approach is conceivable if we assume that both s and v can assume any values between a minimum of zero and some maximum S or V, meaning that s and v are considered as continuous variables. Instead of the matrix of Table 5.I we would then use a two-dimensional frequency distribution with densities $\phi(s, v)$, and total manpower could then be written as an integral,

$$1 = \int_0^S \mathrm{d}s \int_0^V \mathrm{d}v \, \phi(s, v). \tag{5.1}$$

Such a procedure might be fruitful if ϕ can be written as a not too complicated function of s and v, for instance, as the normal or the log-normal distribution. Moreover, the productive contribution of the element $\phi(s, v) \, \mathrm{d}s \, \mathrm{d}v$ should be known explicitly and be close to a not too complicated function of s and v. Exercises with figures for a number of production sectors did not disclose a simple shape for either of these functions and discouraged B. Herman and myself from following this procedure. These exercises actually referred to the two production factors of capital (including human capital) and ('pure', that is, unskilled) labour. In the present essay I therefore stuck to the much simpler discrete-value system expressed in Table 5.I.

5.2. Two alternative Cobb–Douglas production functions

In a first attempt [63] to use a Cobb–Douglas-like production function in ϕ_{sv} I introduced (for two values of s and v each) the function

$$y = C\phi_{11}^{\rho_{11}} \phi_{12}^{\rho_{12}} \phi_{21}^{\rho_{21}} \phi_{22}^{\rho_{22}}. \tag{5.2}$$

This function has the inconvenience that $y = 0$ for ϕ_{12} or $\phi_{21} = 0$, which is completely unrealistic and the function (5.2) has therefore to be rejected. As factors (in the mathematical meaning of that term) we have to introduce sums of ϕ's of either the same s or the same v. Accordingly, in the case described by our Table 5.I, two alternatives can be formulated. If we combine ϕ's with the same s we consider as one production factor the group of people having the same job; if we combine ϕ's with the same v we consider as one production factor the group of people with the same education. In both cases we cannot simply take the unweighted sums, that is, either $\phi_{21} + \phi_{22}$ or $\phi_{11} + \phi_{21}$, since the productivity of an individual with an education not intended for the job will differ from the productivity of an individual with the appropriate level of education for the job considered. Of the two alternatives the former seems better if data are available about incomes by jobs (or job groups), whereas the latter is to be preferred if data are available on incomes by education received. An additional condition for the application of the former alternative is that jobs are classified according to education required. The absence of this sort of data for most countries made me choose in favour of the second alternative, implying the production function as specified in equation (5.3),

$$ y = C(\phi_{11} + \pi_{21}\phi_{21})^{\rho_1}(\phi_{22} + \pi_{32}\phi_{32})^{\rho_2}\phi_{33}^{\rho_3}. \quad (5.3) $$

Here π_{21} constitutes the productivity ratio between individuals with education 1 on jobs 2 and 1; and π_{32}, that ratio between persons with education 2 on jobs 3 and 2. Both π will be > 1, with an upper limit such that the (marginal) productivity on job 2 of an individual with education 1 will be lower than, or at most equal to the (marginal) productivity of an individual with education 2. These assumptions were also made in a previous article on the same subject [63].

In addition I assume that, in a configuration with a very small ϕ_{21}, π_{21} will be very little above 1 and similarly for ϕ_{32} and π_{32}. This assumption is based on the underlying assumption that in reality job 1 stands for a group of jobs, of which the most productive one is very close to the least productive job belonging to group 2. It has to be admitted that a more precise elaboration of this point of view would be useful.

In (5.3) the value of C depends on the units chosen for y and for labour as well as on the contribution to production by capital. Also the sum total of the ρ's equals the portion of national product to be attributed to labour. For the Netherlands the contribution of capital to national product has been taken as equal to 0.2, implying that $\rho_1 + \rho_2 + \rho_3 = 0.8$. For 1962 I estimated $\rho_1 = 0.648$, $\rho_2 = 0.088$ and $\rho_3 = 0.064$. Expressing y in thousands of guilders per employed person I found $C = 15$ and y close to 9.1.

The use of a (generalized) Cobb–Douglas production function implies a choice among many different forms available, differing mainly in the degree of substitutability of the factors of production considered. In most of the more sophisticated studies of production functions now available, using only the quantity and the quality of labour and capital, more complicated forms such as the CES function or even a variable elasticity of substitution have been preferred. In quite a few cases, however, elasticities close to one have been found. Since we want to concentrate on the implications of our distinction between schooling available and schooling required we stick to a Cobb–Douglas function of the form shown, which implies some characteristics of the degree of substitutability between different types of labour. Education planning, during its short period of life, has mostly assumed a low degree of substitution possibility; as an approximation, a fixed mix of the types of labour as characterized by its education, was often assumed, similar to the assumption that for many industries there is a fixed ratio between the quantities of capital and labour. For many industries in fact the substitution of capital for labour or vice versa was shown to be difficult (cf. Boon [4]). Studies on income distribution were mostly based on the assumption of more flexibility in the ratios between the quantities of different types of labour used; partly, however, because of *indirect substitution*, that is, because of the possibilities of changing the industry mix of a country over time or

of different mixes prevailing in countries with different endow-
ments of capital per head.

The need for better knowledge of substitution is now being
felt by both groups of economists mentioned; a usual measure
for substitution possibilities is the substitution elasticity. In
this section the demand substitution elasticity is the one that
will be discussed. The substitution elasticity on the side of the
supply of different types of labour has been discussed elsewhere, for instance by Freeman [24], by the human capital
school [44] and by this author [67].

5.3. Two types of substitution elasticity of demand

An important preliminary question to be answered first is in
what way various types of labour have to be defined. In order
to estimate the demand elasticity of types of labour the
economist will tend to follow the categorization of labour used
by statisticians. This can be found, first of all, in census figures,
and for some countries also in income distribution figures,
whether taken from tax statistics or from special sample
surveys.

Census figures provide, first of all, a broad, one-digit classification, and in addition, finer subdivisions. The trouble with
this classification is, however, that it is based on two principles,
and as yet not shown in a two-entry table or matrix. One
principle is a subdivision of people according to *education
received* (for instance in the categories professionals and
technicians); the other principle is the *type of work* done (as in
the categories administrators and managers). For the description of the population according to education received extensive statistics are available, but these do not mention the type
of work done (cf. also [49]). In tax statistics we now find, for
quite a few countries, incomes according to job categories,
but no data on education received.

As a consequence of this state of affairs, the classifications
used in some recent empirical research suffer from this duality
in census surveys.

In the preceding section I tried to use an, admittedly very crude, two-dimensional classification of income earners, making an explicit distinction between the *job* performed and the *education* received. To be sure, the jobs were defined by the education required, but it was assumed, I think realistically, that education required and education received, are not necessarily identical.

Once this two-dimensionality is assumed, we can distinguish *two different types of substitution*. The first and most usual one is the substitution, for a given job, of a person with one type of education for a person with another type of education. Here we expect the elasticity σ of substitution to be negative; if a category of given education becomes 'cheaper', the organizer of production will exert a larger demand for it, with the limiting case of no change in demand for production with a rigid mix of persons with different levels of education. The *'education substitution elasticity'* is expected to be negative (cf. [69]).

In the second type of substitution, where a person of given education is considered for a job requiring higher education than the job he had so far, he will become more productive (although not as productive as those educated for that higher job). The change in quantity of labour in the new job will then be positive (one man more), and also the change in wage, giving a positive *'job substitution elasticity'*.

The reader may wonder whether the above argument is not too simple, since only one quantity of labour and one price are supposed to change, whereas substitution elasticities refer to the relative changes of two quantities and prices. For simplicity's sake we have kept constant, however, the quantities and prices of the original positions; and so the relative changes have the same sign as the absolute changes in the new positions. In the subsequent section the precise calculations will be shown.

What I want to emphasize here is the essential difference between the two types of substitution and the difference to be expected in the *algebraic signs* of these two types.

A simple example will now be given where the two elasticities of substitution just discussed are computed. The production function used is that of (5.3),

$$y = 15(\phi_{11} + \pi_{21}\phi_{21})^{0.648}(\phi_{22} + \pi_{32}\phi_{32})^{0.088}\phi_{33}^{0.064},$$

(5.4)

where the $\phi_{hh'}$ are the frequencies already defined, y is total national product (including the share of capital) per member of the labour force, and the figures are constants found for the Netherlands in 1962.

The production function could be called semi-empirical since its mathematical form was assumed *a priori*, but the figures were then derived from statistical evidence.

The coefficients π_{21} and π_{32} (assumed to be $1 + 2.3\phi_{21}$ and $1 + 5\phi_{32}$ respectively, if the equilibrium values of ϕ_{21} and ϕ_{32} change) need somewhat further explanation. They represent productivity ratios between the groups 21 and 11, and 32 and 22, respectively. For the individual production organizer they are considered constants, just as in the theory of a competitive market prices are considered given by the individual buyer or seller. As a consequence of the joint action of all individuals ϕ's may change in the longer run; and then π_{21} and π_{32} also change, in the way indicated. The formulae for this change have been chosen in such a way that π_{21} becomes 1 for $\phi_{21} = 0$ and π_{32} becomes 1 for $\phi_{32} = 0$, as already observed in the preceding section.

5.4. Short-term elasticities of substitution

Corresponding to this difference between short-term or microeconomic constancy of the π's and long-term or macroeconomic variation of them, a set of two values can be calculated for each of the elasticities. The first is valid for individual decisions of competing production managers, and the second for central planning of government measures.

Let us now calculate the two elasticities of substitution, and begin with the *short-run* elasticities. As an illustration of the substitution in a given job 2 of a person with education 1 for a person with education 2, we suppose a change in ϕ_{21} and constancy of ϕ_{22}. The relevant elasticity σ_e^s now equals the expression

$$\sigma_e^s = d\frac{\phi_{21}}{\phi_{22}} \bigg/ d\frac{l_{21}}{l_{22}} \cdot \frac{l_{21}}{l_{22}} \bigg/ \frac{\phi_{21}}{\phi_{22}}. \tag{5.5}$$

Since the l's are equal to the corresponding marginal productivities, we have

$$l_{21} = \frac{0.648\pi_{21}y}{\phi_{11} + \pi_{21}\phi_{21}}, \tag{5.6}$$

$$l_{22} = \frac{0.088y}{\phi_{22} + \pi_{32}\phi_{32}}, \tag{5.7}$$

and consequently,

$$\frac{l_{21}}{l_{22}} = \frac{7.4\pi_{21}(\phi_{22} + \pi_{32}\phi_{32})}{\phi_{11} + \pi_{21}\phi_{21}}. \tag{5.8}$$

Since the only change is an increase $d\phi_{21}$ in ϕ_{21}, we have

$$d\frac{l_{21}}{l_{22}} = -\frac{7.4\pi_{21}^2(\phi_{22} + \pi_{32}\phi_{32})\,d\phi_{21}}{(\phi_{11} + \pi_{21}\phi_{21})^2}, \tag{5.9}$$

and

$$d\frac{\phi_{21}}{\phi_{22}} = \frac{d\phi_{21}}{\phi_{22}}, \tag{5.10}$$

hence

$$\sigma_e^s = -\frac{\phi_{11} + \pi_{21}\phi_{21}}{\pi_{21}\phi_{21}}. \tag{5.11}$$

This education substitution elasticity turns out to be negative, as expected; and for the numerical values for the Netherlands around 1962, it is equal to

$$-\frac{0.79 + 0.15}{0.15} = -6.3. \tag{5.12}$$

For the computation of the short-run *job* elasticity we again assume ϕ_{21} to change, with ϕ_{11} constant. The job elasticity σ_j^s will be

$$\sigma_j^s = \mathrm{d}\frac{\phi_{21}}{\phi_{11}} \bigg/ \mathrm{d}\frac{l_{21}}{l_{11}} \cdot \frac{l_{21}}{l_{11}} \bigg/ \frac{\phi_{21}}{\phi_{11}}. \tag{5.13}$$

Since $l_{21}/l_{11} = \pi_{21}$, we have

$$\sigma_j^s = \frac{\mathrm{d}\phi_{21}}{\mathrm{d}\pi_{21}} \frac{\pi_{21}}{\phi_{21}} = \infty. \tag{5.14}$$

5.5. Long-term elasticities of substitution

For the calculation of the *long-run* elasticities we can use formulae (5.8), (5.10) and (5.13), taking into account now that also π varies. *The education elasticity* now has to be obtained from

$$\mathrm{d}\frac{l_{21}}{l_{22}} = \frac{7.4(\phi_{22} + \pi_{32})\,\mathrm{d}\pi_{21}}{\phi_{11} + \pi_{21}\phi_{21}}$$

$$- \frac{7.4\pi_{21}(\phi_{22} + \pi_{32}\phi_{32})(\pi_{21}\mathrm{d}\phi_{21} + \phi_{21}\mathrm{d}\pi_{21})}{(\phi_{11} + \pi_{21}\phi_{21})^2} \tag{5.15}$$

from which we obtain

$$\sigma_e^l = \frac{(\phi_{11} + \pi_{21}\phi_{21})\pi_{21}}{\phi_{21}\{(\phi_{11} + \pi_{21}\phi_{21})\alpha_1 - \pi_{21}^2 - \alpha_1\pi_{21}\phi_{21}\}}. \tag{5.16}$$

This expression *will not always be negative;* in fact for the Netherlands we found it to be, for substitution between education levels 1 and 2, ca 50.

This finding is somewhat paradoxical: why would the planner of production be willing to pay a higher wage when he puts more people with education 1 on jobs requiring education 2? In as far as our model (that is, production function) is correct, he does so because the additional (21) people are taken for lack of (22) people (whose education is geared to the jobs); and he engages the additional (21) people for more difficult jobs, having a higher productivity: π_{21} rises with ϕ_{21}. Since the expression in the denominator of dl_{21} also contains negative terms, which reflect the forces economists ordinarily emphasize, these latter have not been neglected and are even preponderant in our case of substituting education 3 for education 2 or vice versa.

For substitution between levels 2 and 3, we found, indeed, $\sigma_e^l = -2.1$.

The long-term *job elasticity* can be found as follows:

$$\sigma_j^l = d\frac{\phi_{21}}{\phi_{11}} \Big/ d\frac{l_{21}}{l_{11}} \cdot \frac{l_{21}}{l_{11}} \Big/ \frac{\phi_{21}}{\phi_{11}} = \frac{1 + \alpha_1\phi_{21}}{\alpha_1\phi_{21}}. \tag{5.17}$$

For the Dutch figures for the substitution of job 2 for job 1, we found this elasticity to be 15; for the substitution of job 2 for job 3 it became 7.7.

Summarizing our numerical results for the semi-empirical case considered we give, in Table 5.II, a survey.

Table 5.II

Short-term and long-term education and job demand elasticities of substitution between labour of different kinds.

	Levels of substitution			
	Short-term		Long-term	
	1 vs 2	2 vs 3	1 vs 2	2 vs 3
Education elasticities	−6.3	−1.9	50	−2.1
Job elasticities	∞	∞	15	7.7

Comparing these results with some empirical figures mentioned by Psacharopoulos and Hinchliffe [52], our short-term education substitution elasticities are very close to theirs; they find −4.8 and −2.2 (minus sign added by me because of the difference in algebraic sign between their and my definition). They add an elasticity of substitution between persons with primary and without any education; but this figure of -50 is highly uncertain: if we add or subtract one standard deviation from their regression coefficient we obtain elasticity values of -13 and $+29$, respectively.

5.6. Statistical estimation of the elasticity of substitution between graduate and other labour: introductory remarks

As a test of the generalized Cobb–Douglas production function in Sections 5.2–5.5 statistical estimates will be discussed of the demand elasticity of substitution, in national production, between third-level educated or graduate labour and other labour. This elasticity has been chosen because it refers to the only type of labour which has been introduced as a separate category.

For the interstate American material only the highest educational level has been considered third-level (more than 3 years college).

For a clear analysis of the problems of substitution between various labour types, substitution on the demand side – exerted by the organizers of production in the widest sense – should be distinguished, as we already said in Chapter 3, from substitution on the supply side, where many individuals have a choice within a range of occupations. Their willingness to change their job will be determined by their preference functions in which not only the income attached to each of the possible jobs enters, but also the satisfaction or dissatisfaction going with each job. In part, this satisfaction (positive or negative) will depend on each persons' level of education. This, by the way, implies the desirability of describing an individual's position vis-à-vis his or her job with at least two indicators, one for the education required to do the job adequately and one for the education actually received, as set out in the preceding sections.

Some of the authors quoted give more explicit attention to this difference between demand side and supply side than others and some remarks on their methods will be made later (cf. Section 5.7).

This author was struck by the high elasticity figures obtained by several others and wondered how to interpret them. Since the question is of particular relevance to the credibility of some calculations, to be presented in Chapters 6 and 7, on the possibilities of reducing income differences, a few alternative attempts were undertaken, using, among other material, quite a few figures collected by Messrs. Bowles and Dougherty. I am particularly grateful to Dr. Dougherty who most generously provided me with a vast amount of material collected by him [22].

The question whether one can determine, with the aid of figures on *prices* and *quantities* exchanged, the demand or the supply function is an old one; various aspects of it were discussed by Frisch in 1933 [25]. It is irrelevant whether prices and quantities refer to one commodity or to the ratios between two commodities; in fact, the price of one commodity is a price ratio for the price of that good relative to the price of money. The simplest illustration of the dilemma is the situation in which both the supply and the demand curve (or line) in the price–quantity diagram have shifted in one direction. The observed points are then not lying on the demand or on the supply curve but on the '*historical path*', the slope of which can be anything. Another possible situation for which the same conclusion applies is the one of random shifts dealt with by Frisch.

There are various ways out of the dilemma. One is that only one of the curves has shifted; then the observed points are all situated on the other curve. This is what Bowles, Dougherty, Psacharopoulos and Ullman have assumed, in order to estimate the short-term demand curve. The elasticities found in this way are reliable only, however, if the correlation coefficient between the price variable and the quantity variable is high; otherwise the regression coefficient found highly depends on whether the first or the second regression has been determined. Our authors take the regression where the quantities are assumed to be given and the price ratios dependent. For a short-term demand curve this can be accepted, but for a long-term demand function this choice is debatable.

Typically *short-term* reactions are reactions where not only the numbers of people employed, but also and especially, the durable production equipment cannot be changed. As a complement, long-term reactions will contain *changes in industries* and in *technology*. It seems natural to me that in the latter type of decisions the organizers of production will start from their information on prices of products as well as production factors, including those of the various types of labour. For this reason I submit that, for long-run studies, relative quantities also on the demand side should be considered to be the dependent and not the independent variables; of course there will not be a large difference between the alternative results whenever a correlation coefficient close to 1 is obtained. This appears not to be so in the cases of simple correlation presented by two of our authors. Since Bowles' simple correlation coefficient is -0.55 and Dougherty's -0.42, their elasticities would have to be multiplied by $0.55^2 = 0.30$ and $0.42^2 = 0.176$, respectively, if the other simple regression had been taken. This drastically reduces the elasticities.

Another way of solving the dilemma is to add at least one more independent variable to each of the equations linking price and quantity variables. As already observed in Chapter 3, these additional variables have often been called *demand* or *supply 'factors'*; they are supposed to co-determine the quantities actually exchanged, looked at from the demand or the supply side, respectively. Both Bowles and Ullman apply this method; Bowles adds, on the demand side, the percentage of active population in agriculture. Ullman, on the demand side, adds the qualities of the types of labour, represented by dummies for the human capital invested in each individual of the two categories – certainly a highly interesting enrichment –; and on the supply side she adds income and cost of education. Bowles' elasticity of demand reduces from 8 to 6 for the substitution between second- and third-level on the one hand

and lower-level manpower on the other hand; the correlation coefficient (for this substitution) improves from 0.85 to 0.90. For the substitution between third-level educated labour only and all other labour, I calculated, from his figures, but using another additional independent variable (cf. below), an improvement from 0.55 to 0.9.

A third way of separating the demand and supply equation consists of introducing a *time lag* for one of the relations (or a different time lag for both). Clearly this only makes sense if such a lag actually exists and is of sufficient length. For the supply of university graduates this is not an unrealistic assumption and was successfully applied by Freeman for college-trained technicians. Such a lag implies the development over time as shown in the *cobweb theorem*. Fluctuations of this kind are common to coffee, pigs and graduates, probably *bien étonnés de se trouver ensemble*!

5.7. Alternative results from Bowles' (cross-nation) and Dougherty's (cross-state) material

Since for income inequality reduction the substitution of third-level educated manpower (or womanpower, for that matter) by all others is more relevant than any other substitution (as far as I experienced in my attempts in [67]), I tried to derive the relevant long-term demand and supply elasticities from the two relations: *

Demand:

$$\frac{L_1 + L_2}{L_3} = b_1 \frac{w_1 + w_2}{w_3} + b_2 u + b_3, \tag{5.18}$$

Supply:

$$\frac{L_1 + L_2}{L_3} = a_1 \frac{w_1 + w_2}{w_3} + a_2 L_2 + a_3. \tag{5.19}$$

* For the cross-nation material the shape chosen here gives a much better fit than a linear relation between the inverse quantity and price ratios. This does not apply to Dougherty's material.

Here L_i (in Bowles' notation) stands for the labour force with education i, w_i for earnings of category i; $i = 3$ stands for more than 11 years of schooling, which is an overestimation of L_3 and an underestimation of w_3, in comparison to my own approaches. Further, u stands for the per mille of the active population in utilities, health services, transportation and communication (ISIC 5 and 7); this is admittedly an incomplete measure of the services sector, since education and government are not included. The a and b are regression coefficients and their values, together with the corresponding standard deviations (∗), elasticities (ε) and corrected multiple correlation coefficients ($\overline{R}$) are given in Table 5.III. The upper half of the table gives coefficients estimated with the aid of the least-squares method for (5.18) and (5.19) in succession, the lower half gives coefficients estimated with the aid of reduced-form equations.

Table 5.III
Values found for coefficients in (5.18) and (5.19), c, standard deviations ∗ and elasticities ε.

	a_1	a_2	a_3	$\overline{R}_{\text{sup}}$	b_1	b_2	b_3	$\overline{R}_{\text{dem}}$
c	−12	−0.236	33.2	0.70	−14.3	−0.375	48.7	0.89
∗	(9)	(0.095)	(8.7)		(5.6)	(0.070)	(6.2)	
ε	−1	−1			−1.2			
c	109	−0.68		$R_p = 0.47$	−7.1	−0.35		$R_q = 0.85$
ε	8.5				−0.6			

Note: R_p and R_q are multiple correlation coefficients for price and quantity equations.

According to the least-squares estimates the supply elasticity is not significantly different from 0; since its algebraic sign is negative, it may be interpreted as a small consumptive aspect of supply but does not leave much room for the investment in human capital aspect. The theory behind the L_2 term is that in countries with a large number of people with secondary education one has a stronger tendency to be induced to continue one's education. The algebraic sign of a_2 implies no rejection of this theory. The demand equation, in which we are mainly interested, behaves according to expectations: both signs are correct and the values of the coefficients are significant at the 1 per cent level. The corrected multiple correlation coefficient is satisfactory. The demand elasticity is not significantly different from unity, implying support for the generalized Cobb–Douglas production function used in my earlier models.

The reduced-form estimates yield a strongly positive supply elasticity and a demand elasticity half as low even as the least-squares estimate. The multiple correlation coefficients of the price equation (R_p) and the quantity equation (R_q) – both using the demand factor and the supply factor as explanatory variables – are 0.47 and 0.85, respectively.

I applied a similar procedure to the cross-section material collected mainly by Dougherty for the 28 most populous American states.

The relative employment figure now used was the per millage of effective employment in the experienced labour force in 1959 (equivalent males) with third-level education; the relative income figure was the ratio of third-level mean income of males aged 25–64 in the experienced labour force to median income. As the additional supply factor I introduced the median years of schooling S (instead of L_2 in Bowles' case), taken from the US Summary of the 1960 Census of Population; as the additional demand factor v I used the percentage of the active population employed in transportation, etc., finance, professional services and public administration, from Table 128 of the State Volumes of the 1960 Census.

The results of the regression analysis applied to these data are given in Table 5.IV, where the upper half again gives the estimates obtained by least squares applied to the supply and demand equation and the lower half those obtained from reduced-form estimation. In the upper half for the demand equation also the coefficients have been added which were obtained when price ratios are considered the dependent variable.

Table 5.IV
Values found for coefficients for US states, c, standard deviations $*$ and elasticities ε.

	a_1	a_2	a_3	$\bar{R}_{sup}$	b_1	b_2	b_3	$\bar{R}_{dem}$
c	24.0	23.8	-186.6	0.81	-17.9	3.58	69.1	0.72
$*$	(9.9)	(4.0)			(7.0)	(0.86)		
ε	0.54				-0.40			
c					-94	2.42	28.3	0.45
ε					-2.1			
c	11.7	5.35			-3.78	3.30		
ε	2.64			$R_p = 0.80$	-0.85			$R_q = 0.85$

Note : R_p, R_q, cf. Table 5.III.

From the table we see that this time the multiple correlation coefficients obtained for both the price and the quantity equations are rather satisfactory. The demand elasticity obtained from the second demand equation (where price ratios were considered dependent) is -2.1 which comes closer to the Ullman figure of -2.5; but the reduced-form estimate remains (as an absolute figure) below 1. The conclusion seems warranted that the generalized Cobb–Douglas function used in my earlier estimations gives a realistic picture for the substitution elasticity between third-level educated and all other manpower.

6

The race between technological development and education

6.1. Does growth automatically reduce income inequality?

We are now in a position to set out more accurately the long-term results of the interaction of demand for and supply of productive services, in particular some main types of labour. In this chapter we will concentrate on the *long-term movements in income inequality in developed countries*. As already shown with the aid of observed facts in Chapter 2, the main trend in income distribution in developed countries has been toward less inequality. This has even led some commentators and politicians to suggest that with increasing average income inequality goes down *automatically*. Some economists also have expressed this feeling. Kuznets [38] is more cautious and rightly states (p. 212):

'A variety of factors can be discerned, some inducing movements in one direction, others pushing the process in the opposite direction. The resulting trends are a net balance of these conflicting effects of different factors and can properly be explained only if each factor is observed and its possibly changing effects gauged over the period covered.'

In this chapter the factors we propose to deal with are the main demand and supply factors we have so far introduced. On the demand side it is the production function and more particularly the exponent ρ_3 of the number of third-level educated persons. On the supply side it is the proportion x_3 of the labour force which actually has third-level education.

The role played by these two key factors in explaining income inequality will be set out in the following sections. In the choice made among the available demand and supply factors it is implied that the measure of inequality chosen is the ratio of income of university graduates from their labour to the economy's average income.

6.2. Long-term characteristics of demand for university graduates

For a study of long-term developments in income inequality it cannot be assumed that the production function has constant coefficients. In the Cobb–Douglas production function so far used the coefficient ρ_3 stands for the proportion of national product produced by university graduates. This proportion changes for two reasons – the increase in capital and in technological development. In our generalized Cobb–Douglas approach we will accept the statistical fact that the proportion of national income allocated to capital has changed in the long run as is brought out by the figures in Table 6.I, derived from Kuznets [38] pp. 168/9. For comparison a figure of 37 per cent for Colombia, 1966, may be quoted from Jaksch [32].

Table 6.I
Percentage share of capital in national income; various countries and periods.

GB	Share	F	Share	D	Share	USA	Share
1860–69	44	1853	36	1895	35	1899–1908	28
1954–60	24	1954–60	18	1954–60	25	1954–60	21

Note: Figures shown are averages of Kuznets' two alternatives.

Our further calculations will be concentrated on the United States and the Netherlands, since the additional and most relevant information needed is available for these two countries. For the United States a study by Ullman [74] enables us to estimate, for the period 1900–1963, the proportion ρ_3 of national income allocated to the higher educated labour force. Her concept of higher education is wider than only university graduates but we assume that the latter have been a constant portion of the former. Using the following symbols:

η ratio of total income of higher educated to that of others;
ρ_0 portion of national income allocated to capital (Kuznets);
$\bar{\rho}_3$ portion of Ullman's higher educated in national income;
ρ_3 portion of those with more than 16 years of schooling;
y income per capita in the USA in 1960 \$;

we derive from Ullman's figures Table 6.II.

Table 6.II
Figures on income distribution; USA, 1900–1963.

Year	η	ρ_0	$\bar{\rho}_3$ $\left(= \dfrac{\eta(1 - \rho_0)}{1 + \eta}\right)$	ρ_3 $(= 0.27\,\bar{\rho}_3)$	Y^a
1900	0.193	0.28	0.116	0.031	1480
1910	0.280	0.28	0.158	0.043	1720
1920	0.285	0.29	0.158	0.043	2500
1930	0.313	0.30	0.166	0.045	2510
1940	0.411	0.27	0.213	0.057	2500
1948	0.312	0.24	0.181	0.049	3520[b]
1955	0.430	0.21	0.236	0.064	.
1958	0.580	0.21	0.289	0.078	3710[c]
1963	0.610	0.19	0.298	0.081	.

[a] Estimated from Trends in developing countries, World Bank, 1973, Table 2.7, assuming price level in 1960 to be 80 per cent of that in 1970.
[b] 1950.
[c] 1960.

The coefficient 0.27, used to estimate ρ_3 from $\bar{\rho}_3$, has been based on the value of ρ_3 for 1959, derived from American Census data [78] (for males 25 to 64 years old in the experienced labour force).

From Table 6.II we see that the portion of national income allocated to higher-educated manpower has shown a rising trend throughout the period. In order to extrapolate values of

ρ_3 until 1990, a regression on income Y per capita in 1960 \$ was estimated with the result,

$$\rho_3' = 0.046 + 18Y \cdot 10^{-6} \qquad (R = 0.83), \qquad (6.1)$$
$$(5)$$

where R is the correlation coefficient and (5) is the standard deviation of the regression coefficient 18.

As a check for five observations in developed countries around 1960 ρ_3 was also regressed on Y; the data are shown in Table 6.III.

Table 6.III
Estimated portion ρ_3 allocated to university-educated manpower in some developed countries around 1960 and income per capita Y in 1960 \$, for year concerned.

Country	Year	ρ_3	Y	Sources for ρ_3
NL	1962	0.064	1430	Nota Inkomensverdeling [48]
CDN	1961	0.065	2100	Census of Canada, Bull. 4.1-1
S	1974[a]	0.079	3200	Husén [31]
USA	1959	0.078	2690	Census of Population, earnings
USA	1968	0.130	3490	Census sample, corrected

[a] Husén's figures refer to 35-year-olds in 1964. They have been taken to represent total working force composition for 1974, since 45 years of age is close to the average age of the labour force.

The cross-section regression equation appears to be

$$\rho_3' = 0.016 + 26Y \cdot 10^{-6} \qquad (R = 0.86). \qquad (6.2)$$
$$(8.2)$$

With the aid of these two regression equations extrapolated values for ρ_3 were obtained, based on alternative values for Y. For 1970–1980 an annual growth rate of 3 per cent and for 1980–1990 two alternatives of 3 and 2 per cent per annum were used. These growth rates are lower than the rate for 1960–1970, which was 3.2 per cent, in order to take into account the probable and necessary deceleration of growth in view of environmental factors, including the increased scarcity of energy and food expected for the world at large [72].

Table 6.IV
Values of ρ_3; USA, 1950–1990.

Year	Eq. (6.1)	Eq. (6.2)
1950	0.090	0.080
1960	0.096	0.088
1970	0.114	0.115
1980	0.138	0.149
1990 high	0.169	0.194
1990 low	0.158	0.178

A similar extrapolation, forward to 1990 and backward to 1900, has been made for the Netherlands. National income per capita at constant prices of 1970 are available from the National Accounts for 1972 over the period 1900–1970 (Netherlands Central Bureau of Statistics). For 1980, income per capita has been estimated at 150 per cent of 1970; this corresponds with 4.1 per cent growth per annum, as opposed to 3.9 per cent between 1960 and 1970 and is accounted for by the sudden fall in birth rates. For 1990 a high estimate has been based on the same rate of growth and a low one based on a 2 per cent annual increase, for the reasons given with regard to the USA. Transformation of the incomes per capita on a 1960 $ basis and the two alternative calculations of ρ_3 are shown in Table 6.V.

Table 6.V
Income per capita, 1970 = 100 and in 1960 $, and calculations of ρ_3 with the aid of formulae (6.1) and (6.2); the Netherlands, 1900–1990.

Year	Income per capita		ρ_3	
	1970 = 100	In 1960 $	Eq. (6.1)	Eq. (6.2)
1900	30	585	0.057	0.032
1930	46	900	0.062	0.039
1960	67	1310	0.070	0.050
1970	100	1940	0.081	0.066
1980	150	2910	0.098	0.092
1990 high	225	4400	0.125	0.130
1990 low	183	3505	0.109	0.107

6.3. Long-term characteristics of supply of university graduates

For both countries figures are available over the period 1900–1990 giving an estimate of the percentage of manpower with university education. For the United States, Ullman's estimates [74] cover a wider category, as already observed, but from 1940 onwards census figures are available which have been extrapolated until 1990 [61]. For the Netherlands, J. Passenier [50] has presented a series for the whole period 1900–1990. Since the overwhelming part of manpower expected to live in 1990 has already been born, there is no demographic reason to work with two alternatives for 1990 on the supply side; but two educational forecasts are given for the USA. The figures for both countries are given in Table 6.VI.

Table 6.VI
Percentage of labour force with higher or university education x_3; USA and the Netherlands, 1900–1990.

	1900	1910	1920	1930	1940	1948	1960	1970	1980	1990
USA higher	7.2	10.7	13.9	13.4	18.0	16.6	31.4[a]			
USA university (low)	1.8	2.7	3.6	3.4	4.6	6.0[b]	7.7	11.0	14.5	18.1
USA university (high)									15.0	20.5
NL university	0.54	–	–	0.61	–	0.88[c]	1.32	1.82	3.33	5.00

[a] Interpolated between 1958 and 1963.
[b] 1950.
[c] 1947.

The main tendency brought out by the figures is the steep increase since 1900, not only in historical figures, but also in expected figures for the last two decades. Even so figures have occasionally fallen. Then, although the figures for the United States must be higher than those of the Netherlands, they are not likely to be so very much higher, as the table shows. Some difference in definition probably remains. In fact, for males between 25 and 64 in 1959 the percentage of the experienced labour force with university education is given as 5.1 (5 or more years of college). For our purpose only the relative rise is important, however, and the inter-country difference should not be taken too literally.

6.4. Impact of the race between technology and education on income inequality

With the aid of the figures given or derived in the two preceding sections we can now estimate the income ratio of university graduates to the average income recipient. With our generalized Cobb–Douglas production function this ratio equals ρ_3/x_3 and these figures are shown in Table 6.VII.

Table 6.VII

Ratio ρ_3/x_3 of income with university training to average income recipients; USA and the Netherlands, with alternatives, 1900–1990.

	Eq. for ρ_3	1900	1930	1950	1960	1970	1980	1990 (low)	1990 (high)
USA	(6.1)	4.05	2.67	1.50	1.25	1.04	0.92–0.95	0.77–0.87	0.83–0.94
USA	(6.2)	3.15	2.38	1.33	1.14	1.04	0.99–1.02	0.87–0.99	0.95–1.07
NL	(6.1)	10.5	10.1		5.3	4.5	2.9	2.2	2.5
NL	(6.2)	5.8	6.4		3.8	3.6	2.8	2.1	2.6

In this table again the absolute figures for both countries are not to be taken seriously, since the ρ_3 have been based, for formula (6.1) on the absolute level for 1959 only, which may have been exceptional, and for formula (6.2) on the values for five countries. In fact, in 1972, family income with a university-trained head was still 150 per cent of average family income; or, alternatively, in 1959 earnings of a university-trained member of the labour force were 190 per cent of the mean earnings. What is significant is the movement over time. For the low 1990 USA figures and for the Netherlands, the *trend is falling consistently*. Only the high figures for 1990, based on a continuation of past growth in income per capita, are an exception: in that case the race between technological development and education *will be lost by education*. Generally, however, in the past 70 years that race has been *won by education* and Ullman's figures show this without the roundabout way of our table, set up for forecasting purposes. If we take the average between high and low figures for 1990, they tell us that between 1970 and 1990 our inequality index (ratio between income from university training and average income) pre-

sumably will fall by another 18 per cent according to formula
(6.1) and by 7 per cent according to formula (6.2) after having
fallen, between 1900 and 1970, by 74 and 67 per cent, respectively. For the Netherlands a further reduction by 48 and 35
per cent, respectively, is forecast, after a reduction from 1900
to 1970 by 57 and 38 per cent, respectively. The divergencies
between the alternatives illustrate the uncertainties involved.
Even so, it stands to reason that more possibilities for a further
reduction exist in the Netherlands than in the United States.
Finally the reader must be reminded of the fact that this
chapter deals with *primary incomes.* Incomes after redistribution show a much less unequal picture, as illustrated in
Chapter 2. This aspect will be taken up again in the subsequent
chapters.

6.5. Irrelevance of concepts of surplus or shortage of university graduates

With the strong increase in the number of university-trained
workers extensive discussions have developed about the
question whether or not '*too many*' *university-trained* individuals have been delivered by the educational system and
whether, consequently, educational policies should not be
changed so as to prevent these larger numbers of university
graduates from entering the labour market. Calculations have
been presented concerning 'the' demand for various types of
university graduates, often in an attempt to show that the
market is 'flooded' with many types of graduates for whom
employment 'néver' will be found. Similarly, at the other end
of the labour market unskilled labour is said to be in serious
shortage and foreign workers have to be attracted, since the
national labour force is no longer prepared to do the dirty or
otherwise hard work.

Such statements tend to create considerable misunderstanding about the nature of the problems concerned. In the short
run the situation may be represented more or less correctly
by the expressions and statements quoted. For the long-run

development they are *irrelevant* and the operation of the price mechanism is neglected. The school of education planners, mentioned in Section 1.2 and in Chapter 5, has rightly understood that demand for practically all types of manpower is not rigid but depends on the price to be paid. Similarly the human capital school has correctly based its analysis of supply on the incomes to be expected.

From the figures shown in this chapter we see that the percentage of manpower with higher education has risen fourfold between 1900 and 1960 in the United States and trebled between 1900 and 1965 in the Netherlands. On occasions when the demand for unskilled labour has risen considerably, as for instance in the Punjab in India as a consequence of the 'green revolution', its wages have trebled within a few years. If unskilled jobs paid better than they pay at present in Europe, quite a few foreign workers could be replaced by nationals again. This is not to say that such a substitution is desirable before unemployment in the home countries of the foreign workers has been eliminated. The point is, however, that there is *no pre-ordained wage ratio* between skilled and unskilled workers or any other type of labour, and that too often public discussion on income and education policies tend to overlook this.

7

Actual, feasible and optimal income distribution

7.1. Complete models for the Netherlands around 1962

The utility and production functions discussed in Chapters 4 and 5 enable us to build a more complete model than the partial one used in Chapter 6 to illustrate a major dynamic feature of our income distribution theory. This *more complete model* (Section 7.2) will contain all five types of labour introduced in Chapter 5 and enable us to study the effect of some *changes in data* on frequencies and incomes (and hence their distribution) of all five groups. To begin with, in Section 7.3 we will vary the numbers of persons with first-, second- and third-level education; and if these are feasible, the model will show the consequences for incomes. In Section 7.4, the effects of changes in *taxes* and in *technology*, the latter as treated in Chapter 6, will be studied. Next, in Section 7.5, we will postulate a social welfare function, specifying it as the sum of all personal welfare, and inquire as to what the *optimal* income distribution looks like. Whereas in the first exercise *taxes* will be considered given, in the second problem they will be considered unknown and will result from the optimization process. Finally, in Section 7.6, we return to our 21-group Dutch job–education groups and to our American data of Chapter 4, in order to illustrate our concept of optimality in income distribution in some more detail (cf. also [68]).

In the present chapter education *required* will be indicated by h (taking values of 1, 2 or 3) and education *supplied* by h' (also taking these three values).

The utility functions used have been described in Chapter 4, but using other units for education levels. Adapted to our units they become for the Netherlands around 1962,

$$\omega_{hh'} = \ln\{x_{hh'} - 0.90h + c_1 h' - 0.64(h - h')^2\},$$
(7.1)

where we will take $c_1 = 0$ for reasons indicated in Section 4.2.

7.2. The complete analytical model

As set out in Chapter 5, equation (5.4), we have chosen a Cobb–Douglas-like production function,

$$y = 15(\phi_{11} + \pi_{21}\phi_{21})^{0.648}(\phi_{22} + \pi_{32}\phi_{32})^{0.088}\phi_{33}^{0.064}, \quad (7.2)$$

with y being expressed in thousands of guilders (of around 1962) per capita of the labour force and a capital income equal to 20 per cent of total income. The exponents represent the *shares* in total income of the labour force with, respectively, levels 1, 2 and 3 of actual education; therefore the exponents add up to 0.80. The expressions in parentheses represent these components of the labour force, taking into account that the *productivity* of an individual with education level 1 on a job requiring level 2 will be higher by a factor π_{21} than an individual $(1, 1)$'s productivity; and similarly for the labour force $(3, 2)$. While in a given situation of society as a whole, individuals will consider π_{21} and π_{32} as given and constant while making their choices, the values of the π are linked to those of the ϕ, according to the following rules:

$$\pi_{21} = 1 + \alpha_1\phi_{21} \quad \text{as long as} \quad l_{21} < l_{22}, \quad (7.3)$$

$$\pi_{32} = 1 + \alpha_2\phi_{32} \quad \text{as long as} \quad l_{32} < l_{33}, \quad (7.4)$$

where $\alpha_1 = 2.3$ and $\alpha_2 = 5.0$ and the l's represent the marginal productivities (and hence *primary* incomes) of the groups concerned. If l_{21} reaches the level l_{22}, relation (7.3) will no longer be valid, and will be replaced by

$$l_{21} = l_{22}, \quad (7.3')$$

similarly for (7.4),

$$l_{32} = l_{33}. \tag{7.4'}$$

The values for α_1 and α_2 have been derived from the statistical material available. *Marginal productivities* will be, as usual for a Cobb–Douglas production function,

$$l_{11} = \frac{0.648y}{\phi_{11} + \pi_{21}\phi_{21}}, \tag{7.5}$$

$$l_{21} = \frac{0.648\pi_{21}y}{\phi_{11} + \pi_{21}\phi_{21}}, \tag{7.6}$$

$$l_{22} = \frac{0.088y}{\phi_{22} + \pi_{32}\phi_{32}}, \tag{7.7}$$

$$l_{32} = \frac{0.088\pi_{32}y}{\phi_{22} + \pi_{32}\phi_{32}}, \tag{7.8}$$

$$l_{33} = \frac{0.064y}{\phi_{33}}. \tag{7.9}$$

These equations represent the *demand* equations for abilities (11), (21), (22), (32) and (33). With the aid of (7.3) and (7.4) they can also be used to express the ϕ explicitly in terms of the l.

An *analytical* model for us is that version of the model most appropriate for solving the analytical problem, that is, expressing the target or aim variables in terms of instrument variables, or the variables within the control of government. Among the latter are, to begin with, the tax rates and, up to a point, the distribution of the levels of education 1, 2 and 3 over the active population. This distribution is reflected in the values of F_1, F_2 and F_3, where

$$F_1 = \phi_{11} + \phi_{21}, \tag{7.10}$$

$$F_2 = \phi_{22} + \phi_{32}, \tag{7.11}$$

$$F_3 = \phi_{33}. \tag{7.12}$$

The control of government over these data is limited, however, by the innate qualities of the population which may set upper limits to F_2 and F_3. In this book we will not study these limitations, but only show the consequences of a few different values to be given to the F.

The analytical version of our model appears to have *four subversions:* (i) one in which $\phi_{21} = \phi_{32} = 0$, (ii) or (iii) in which either ϕ_{21} or ϕ_{32} equals zero, and (iv) one where both are $\neq 0$. In all subversions equations (7.2) and (7.5) through (7.12) must be fulfilled. In case (iv) we have, in addition, deduced from (7.1),

$$x_{11} - 0.9 = x_{21} - 1.8 - 0.64, \tag{7.13}$$

$$x_{22} - 1.8 = x_{32} - 2.7 - 0.64. \tag{7.14}$$

For subversion (i) the latter two equations become inequalities,

$$x_{11} - 0.9 > x_{21} - 1.8 - 0.64, \tag{7.13'}$$

and

$$x_{22} - 1.8 > x_{32} - 2.7 - 0.64. \tag{7.14'}$$

In subversion (ii) equations (7.13') and (7.14) and in subversion (iii) (7.13) and (7.14') must be satisfied. Inequality (7.13') expresses that for individuals with education 1 it is preferable to have a job 1 than to have a job 2 and that hence $\phi_{21} = 0$; similarly for (7.14') and $\phi_{32} = 0$.

Finally in the analytical version of the model the x will be linked to the l by the relations

$$x_{11} - x_{21} = 0.85 \, (l_{11} - l_{21}), \tag{7.15}$$

and

$$x_{22} - x_{32} = 0.75 \, (l_{22} - l_{32}), \tag{7.16}$$

expressing that a *marginal tax rate* of 0.15 applies to the interval $l_{11} - l_{21}$ and one of 0.25 to the interval $l_{22} - l_{32}$. Clearly these are approximations only, since the marginal tax rates will vary with the levels of l. Upon inspection the approximation is very close, however.

Table 7.I
Analytical model; equations and unknowns of each of the four subversions.

Subversion	Equations		Unknowns[b]
(i) 11^a	$\phi_{21} = \phi_{32} = 0$	(7.2) (7.3) (7.4) (7.5) (7.7) (7.9) (7.10) (7.11) (7.12)	y, 5ϕ, 2π, $3l$
(ii) 13^a	$\phi_{21} = 0$	(7.2) (7.3) (7.4) (7.5) (7.7) (7.8) (7.9) (7.10) (7.11) (7.12) (7.14) (7.16)	y, 5ϕ, 2π, $4l$, $1\Delta x$
(iii) 13^a	$\phi_{32} = 0$	(7.2) (7.3) (7.4) (7.5) (7.6) (7.7) (7.9) (7.10) (7.11) (7.12) (7.13) (7.15)	y, 5ϕ, 2π, $4l$, $1\Delta x$
(iv) 15^a		(7.2) (7.3) (7.4) (7.5) (7.6) (7.7) (7.8) (7.9) (7.10) (7.11) (7.12) (7.13) (7.14) (7.15) (7.16)	y, 5ϕ, 2π, $5l$, $2\Delta x$

[a] This figure indicates the number of unknowns and equations.
[b] 5ϕ means five different ϕ, etc.; Δx means $x_{11} - x_{21}$ or $x_{22} - x_{32}$.

Table 7.I summarizes the equations and the unknowns of each of the four subversions.

7.3. Variation of numbers of persons with education levels 1, 2 and 3

We will not illustrate each of the possible situations, but only subversions (i) and (iv), with some numerical results obtained for the situation originally observed in the Netherlands and for some alternative values of the data F_1, F_2 and F_3. These figures are shown in Table 7.II.

Table 7.II

Changes in incomes and frequencies as a consequence of changes in the total manpower with education levels 1, 2 and 3.

Case Subversion	A (iv)	B (iv)	C (i)	D (i)
F_1	0.91	0.88	0.85	0.81
F_2	0.059	0.08	0.09	0.11
F_3	0.030	0.04	0.06	0.08
ϕ_{21}	0.120	0.12	0.00	.
ϕ_{32}	0.030	0.045	0.00	.
l_{11}	6.2	6.6	6.9	7.35
l_{21}	7.9	8.4	.	.
l_{22}	12.5	9.11	8.9	7.35
l_{32}	14.4	11.15	.	.
l_{33}	21.4	14.90	9.7	7.35
y	9.05	9.31	9.10	9.15

Case D has been chosen on purpose so as to make $F_1 : F_2 : F_3 = 0.648 : 0.088 : 0.064$, that is proportional to the exponents in the production function. As a consequence, $l_{11} = l_{22} = l_{33}$; this will imply tax rates different from the prevailing ones or the ones assumed in equations (7.15) and (7.16). In fact, the *tax equations are not included* in subversion (i); and other tax equations can be added without affecting the figures of cases C and D. Case D has mainly been chosen in order to remind the reader of the fact that a complete equalization of primary incomes does not require all manpower to be of equal qualification, but only to be available in the numbers 'needed' by the production process.

The interesting feature of Table 7.II is that the intermediary cases B and C already show a *substantial decrease in inequality* compared with case A.

7.4. Changes in taxes and technology

The other data – apart from numbers of active persons with the three levels of schooling – appearing in our model are taxes [in subversions (ii), (iii) and (iv)] and the exponents of the production function. As announced in Section 7.1, we will now have a look at the impacts of changes in taxes and in technology on the incomes and income distribution in our model.

To begin with, the *impact of taxes:* this problem is of interest for at least two reasons. First of all, governments have increasingly used taxes in order to arrive at an income distribution different from the one produced by *laissez-faire.* In Chapter 2 extensive statistical information has been presented showing the important differences between (i) primary income distribution, that is, income distribution before taxes are paid, (ii) distribution after taxes and (iii) distribution after complete redistribution, taking into account also the effect of services by the community supplied to consumers at prices below their cost. In this section the incomes after taxes, indicated by the variables x, will be studied in their relation to incomes before taxes, l, especially in order to discover how taxes affect *income distribution.* The second reason for analysing this problem is the importance attached by fiscal experts to the so-called problem of *tax shifting.* The central problem here is whether, and if so to what extent, some groups of the population can avoid the burden of taxation by asking for a higher primary income and actually obtaining it.

The nature of our model permits us to formulate some *general statements* which, however, because of the semi-macro character of our model, do not completely cover the problem.

In addition, the model enables us to make *numerical estimates* of the changes in incomes, primary as well as after tax, caused by given changes in tax rates.

One general statement was already made at the end of the preceding section, where the reader was reminded of the non-occurrence in subversion (i) of the model of any tax variables. The implication is that cases C and D in Table 7.II constitute examples of situations in which *primary incomes are not affected by tax rates.* A transparent situation is in particular the one of D, showing that, if the numbers of active persons with schooling of levels 1, 2 and 3 are proportional to the exponents ρ_1, ρ_2 and ρ_3, primary incomes of the three categories will become equal. Whether this situation can be attained in reality clearly depends on the numbers of students who are able to absorb a secondary and a third-level education. Most developed countries are in the process of experimenting with this possibility: the numbers of students have increased very considerably during the last two decades. As illustrated by the estimates given in Chapter 6, with a time lag of a few decades this process will affect the composition of the labour force and may well reduce primary income inequalities in the coming decades further, as it did during several decades after 1900.

An additional general statement can be made with regard to the other subversions of our model. The only equations needed to calculate primary incomes l are (7.15) and (7.16), and these equations *do not contain full information about the tax system.* On the contrary, *only tax differentials* between groups 11 and 12 and 22 and 32, respectively, enter into these equations, and we can state, therefore, that primary incomes are independent of all other features of the tax system. Primary incomes of people with third-level income are not, therefore, dependent on the tax rates they have to pay themselves. This implies that they cannot shift their taxes. The statement is correct only, of course, under the assumptions on which the model is built. The most important among these assumptions would seem to be:

(i)   Third-level educated manpower is scarce.

(ii) The demand elasticity of substitution between this type of manpower and the other types is unity.

(iii) There is free competition among the organizers of production.

It should be noted that assumption (ii) has been verified statistically and that assumption (iii) does not imply whether or not there is competition *on the supply side* of this compartment of the labour market.

So much about the general statements. Let us now turn to some *numerical estimates* made with the aid of the model. A number of variants were made of case B, characterizing a situation where slightly more people are available with a second- and a third-level education than were present in the Netherlands in 1962. This situation is close to reality and provides realism to our variations as well. The results have been collected in Table 7.III.

Before commenting on the results, some more information about the variations chosen is fitting. Case B' has only been calculated in order to *correct* case B for the small shift in differential tax rates needed in order to take into account the changes in incomes *l* in comparison to case A (Table 7.II). In view of the very minor differences between B and B', the latter was not used for tax variation purposes. Cases B", B''' and B'''' all constitute *attempts to reduce inequality* in incomes *x after tax*. First, taxes *t* were assumed to be a *quadratic function Q* of incomes *l*, as specified in the table. Parameters of the tax schedules have been chosen so as to attain a given total revenue of 1.38 per active person, as collected in 1962. Since these functions were chosen in such a way that the tax *differentials* chosen were approximately in accordance with them, they somewhat miss the point, in that, especially for B" and B''', the *rates* for the lowest income group become higher than for B. The only equalizing effect they have is to reduce income after tax for group 33. Then a broken linear tax function BL was chosen, which indeed brings less inequality for group 11. With a broken linear system one has to see to it that the ranking of incomes after tax remains the same as that of incomes before tax. With regard to groups 32 and 33 this was introduced explicitly. Figures for total product y are averages for all active persons and are in accordance, for case A, with actual 1962 figures.

Table 7.III

Incomes before (l) and after (x) taxes (t) of the five types of labour considered, assuming that 8 per cent of the labour force has secondary and 4 per cent higher education; under various tax systems.

		Case symbols				
		B	B′	B″	B‴	B⁗
Differential tax rates	educ. 1	0.15	0.16	0.10	0.00	0.39
	educ. 2	0.25	0.20	0.25	0.25	0.25
Tax scale[a]		Q_1	n.s.	Q_2	Q_3	BL
Average income y[b]		9.31	9.30	9.29	9.24	9.24
Primary incomes 1000 Dfl.	l_{11}	6.60	6.58	6.63	6.63	6.63
	l_{21}	8.40	8.38	8.30	8.15	8.15
	l_{22}	9.11	9.30	9.10	8.98	8.98
	l_{32}	11.15	11.20	11.18	11.03	11.03
	l_{33}	14.90	14.90	14.86	14.75	14.75
Tax amounts 1000 Dfl.	t_{11}	1.22	.	1.24	1.34	0.975
	t_{21}	1.51	.	1.30	1.34	1.56
	t_{22}	1.65	.	1.44	1.46	2.07
	t_{32}	2.00	.	1.97	2.20	2.58
	t_{33}	2.95	.	3.49	3.88	5.80
Income after taxes 1000 Dfl.	x_{11}	5.4	.	5.39	5.29	5.66
	x_{21}	6.9	.	7.00	6.81	6.59
	x_{22}	7.5	.	7.66	7.52	6.91
	x_{32}	9.0	.	9.21	8.83	8.45
	x_{33}	12.0	.	11.37	10.87	8.95
'Mixed groups'	ϕ_{21}	0.12	0.12	0.11	0.10	0.10
	ϕ_{32}	0.045	0.041	0.045	0.0456	0.456

[a] Q_1 $t = 0.61 + 0.042\,l + 0.0077\,l^2$.   Total tax receipts 1.38.
   Q_2 $t = 2.09 - 0.336\,l + 0.029\ l^2$.   Total tax receipts 1.38.
   Q_3 $t = 3.92 - 0.71\ \ l + 0.048\ l^2$.   Total tax receipts 1.38.
   BL   For $l < 7.5$: $t = 0.975$; for $7.5 < l < 8.5$: $t = 1.56$; for $8.5 < l < 12.5$: $t = 0.25(l - 8.5) + 1.95$; for $12.5 < l$: $t = 0.80\ (l - 12.5) + 4.00$.
  n.s.   Not specified.
[b] y Average income per active person in 1000 Dfl.

The quantitative variations shown in Table 7.III clearly support the extension of our theoretical statement for cases C and D made earlier: *Tax changes have a very slight impact on primary incomes for all five labour categories.* This implies that the impossibility of shifting, found for group 33, also applies in our model to the other 'mixed' groups where education required does not always coincide with actual education. Looked at from the opposite side this implies that redistribution by direct taxes *does constitute a means to reduce inequality,* provided it is applied to a sufficient extent. In the next section it will be shown, however, that *optimal* taxes are taxes which do not depend on income; they depend on capabilities and similar data of the problem, rather than on results of the process of choice of occupation such as income.

The impact of *changes in technology* can be ascertained by repeating the calculations for different values of the exponents ρ. This implies, as already discussed in Chapter 6, that the portions of national income imputed to the three categories of manpower with first-, second- and third-level education change accordingly. As discussed in Chapter 6, technological development tends to raise ρ_3. It seems likely that ρ_1 will fall, whereas the change in ρ_2 remains uncertain. Generally, technological development will tend to widen income differences, *unless a deliberate effort* be made to *direct technological innovation* to more labour-intensive methods in the sense of their requiring more *labour of low education level.* While there seem to be such possibilities, it is outside the scope of this study to enter into more detail here.

7.5. The complete optimalization model

In addition to the analytical model just described a policy model will also be used, in particular, a model for determining the *optimal income distribution.* This model will be set up in the tradition of welfare economics, as a model for *maximizing social welfare* under various restrictions. The social welfare function will be taken equal to the weighted average of individual welfare functions (7.1), the weights being the $\phi_{hh'}$. The restrictions will be (a) the production function (7.2), into which equations (7.3) and (7.4) will be substituted from the start, and the balance equations for (b) labour and for (c) the product.

Two subversions will be considered with regard to labour; subversion (i) will consider as given each of the F_1, F_2 and F_3 separately, whereas subversion (ii) will consider as given only their total, implying that any number of people can absorb education of all types. The balance equations for the product will only express that total product y equals the total of expenditures $x_{hh'}$ by each labour group h, h'. We do not specify whether these are expenditures on consumer or on investment goods, since we are not interested here in development, but rather in income structure. Using Lagrangian multipliers, the problem can be formulated as the determination of the maximum of (i),

$$\phi_{11} \ln(x_{11} - 0.90) + \phi_{21} \ln(x_{21} - 2.44)$$
$$+ \phi_{22} \ln(x_{22} - 1.80) + \phi_{32} \ln(x_{32} - 3.34)$$
$$+ \phi_{33} \ln(x_{33} - 2.70) + \lambda\{y - 15(F_1 + 2.3\phi_{21}^2)^{0.648}$$
$$\times (F_2 + 5\phi_{32}^2)^{0.088} F_3^{0.064}\} + \mu(F_1 - \phi_{11} - \phi_{21})$$
$$+ v(F_2 - \phi_{22} - \phi_{32}) + \pi(F_3 - \phi_{33})$$
$$+ \tau(\phi_{11}x_{11} + \phi_{21}x_{21} + \phi_{22}x_{22} + \phi_{32}x_{32}$$
$$+ \phi_{33}x_{33} - y), \tag{7.17}$$

where for subversion (ii),

$$\mu = v = \pi. \tag{7.18}$$

Differentiation with regard to the eleven variables ϕ, x and y yields

$$\ln(x_{11} - 0.90) - \lambda \frac{0.648y}{F_1 + 2.3\phi_{21}^2} - \mu + \tau x_{11} = 0, \tag{7.19}$$

$$\ln(x_{21} - 2.44) - \lambda \frac{0.648(1 + 2.3\phi_{21})y}{F_1 + 2.3\phi_{21}^2}$$

$$- \mu + \tau x_{21} = 0, \qquad (7.20)$$

$$\ln(x_{22} - 1.80) - \lambda \frac{0.088y}{F_2 + 5\phi_{32}^2} - v + \tau x_{22} = 0, \qquad (7.21)$$

$$\ln(x_{32} - 3.34) - \lambda \frac{0.088(1 + 5\phi_{32})y}{F_2 + 5\phi_{32}^2} - v + \tau x_{32} = 0, \qquad (7.22)$$

$$\ln(x_{33} - 2.70) - \lambda \frac{0.064y}{F_3} - \pi + \tau x_{33} = 0, \qquad (7.23)$$

$$\frac{\phi_{11}}{x_{11} - 0.90} + \tau \phi_{11} = 0, \qquad (7.24)$$

$$\frac{\phi_{21}}{x_{21} - 2.44} + \tau \phi_{21} = 0, \qquad (7.25)$$

$$\frac{\phi_{22}}{x_{22} - 1.80} + \tau \phi_{22} = 0, \qquad (7.26)$$

$$\frac{\phi_{32}}{x_{32} - 3.34} + \tau \phi_{32} = 0, \qquad (7.27)$$

$$\frac{\phi_{33}}{x_{33} - 2.70} + \tau \phi_{33} = 0, \qquad (7.28)$$

$$\lambda - \tau = 0. \qquad (7.29)$$

The solution can be started by the elimination of τ with the aid of (7.29). Equations (7.24) through (7.28) can be satisfied by either (I),

$$x_{11} - 0.90 = x_{21} - 2.44 = x_{22} - 1.80$$

$$= x_{32} - 3.34 = x_{33} - 2.70, \qquad (7.30)$$

or (II),

$$x_{11} - 0.90 = x_{22} - 1.80 = x_{33} - 2.70, \qquad (7.31)$$

together with

$$\phi_{21} = \phi_{32} = 0. \qquad (7.32)$$

Pursuing case (I) we can eliminate μ and v from (7.19) and (7.20), respectively, from (7.21) and (7.22); using (7.30) we then find

$$\phi_{21} = \frac{1.54(F_1 + 2.3\phi_{21}^2)}{0.648 \times 2.3y}, \qquad (7.33)$$

$$\phi_{32} = \frac{1.54(F_2 + 5\phi_{21}^2)}{0.088 \times 5y}. \qquad (7.34)$$

Together with (7.2) we now have three equations in y, ϕ_{21} and ϕ_{32}. It appears possible to solve these non-linear equations numerically. With the initial values $F_1 = 0.911$, $F_2 = 0.059$ and $F_3 = 0.030$ we find the values given in Table 7.IV.

Table 7.IV

Optimal values of variables relevant to income distribution for given values of manpower with first-, second- and third-level education.

Group[a]	l	l^{i} [b]	ϕ	ϕ^{i} [b]	x	t^c	y	y^i [b]
11	6.1	6.2	0.80	0.79	8.6	−2.5		
21	7.7	7.9	0.11	0.12	10.1	−2.4		
22	12.6	12.5	0.035	0.029	9.5	3.1	8.9	9.05
32	14.1	14.4	0.024	0.03	10.8	3.3		
33	19.0	21.4	0.03	0.03	10.4	8.6		

[a] First figure indicates job level; second figure, education level.
[b] Initial values observed for the Netherlands around 1962.
[c] Taxes calculated as $l - x$.

It will be observed that the changes in *primary* incomes – in comparison with the initial situation – are slight only, except for the *highest* income group. The main change takes place in the *redistribution* system. This is seen at once from the tax figures which show two new features. First, negative taxes are required for the two lower groups, those with education level 1. Secondly, taxes do not depend on the job level, but only on the *level of abilities*. Evidently the *feasibility* of the optimum depends on the feasibility of such a tax system, which represents an example of a *lump-sum* tax: the tax rate does not influence the marginal income connected with a change in job and the corresponding income. For the time being a capability tax seems impossible to administer; this would require a refinement in psycho-technical testing which may take a few decades. The need for lump-sum taxes has been understood for a long time [62]. Until they become feasible only second-best solutions to the problem of how to establish an optimum regime, such as income and wealth taxes, can be used.

Let us now take up case (II), where *no limits to education* are assumed to exist. The solution now becomes as shown in Table 7.V.

Table 7.V

Optimal values of variables relevant to income distribution, assuming unlimited capabilities to absorb more education.

Group[a]	l	l^i [b]	ϕ	ϕ^i [b]	x	t^c	y	y^i [b]
11	7.1	6.2	0.835	0.79	8.9	−1.8		
21	.	7.9	0.00	0.12	.	.		
22	8.0	12.5	0.10	0.029	9.8	−1.8	9.15	9.05
32	.	14.4	0.00	0.03	.	.		
33	9.0	21.4	0.065	0.03	10.7	−1.7		

[a] First figure indicates job level; second figure, education level.
[b] Initial values observed for the Netherlands around 1962.
[c] Taxes calculated as $l - x$.

As could be expected, a considerable reduction in income inequality results. Two features of the solution, however, are surprising at first sight. One is that the *number of persons with third-level education* required in this case is *not so large* – it is about double the number prevailing in the initial situation. Also the number required with secondary education is not large at all. With the information now available – that is about ten years after the initial period – the figures for ϕ_{22} and ϕ_{33} do not seem illusory. Before discussing the question why the actual income distribution did not at all change as much as suggested by Table 7.V, we first want to draw attention to the fact that all taxes are now negative. What is the source of these taxes in the model used? It appears to be capital income, which represents, as already observed, 20 per cent of y, which equals 1.8. In the optimum situation capital income is distributed proportionately over the working population.

This feature of our model is less essential, however, than the feature of lump-sum taxes. We could have changed the balance equation for product use by introducing into it public consumption of a given portion of total product, say ψy; this would have changed (7.29) into

$$\lambda - \tau(1 - \psi) = 0, \tag{7.29'}$$

and accordingly reduced the negative taxes by a factor $1 - \psi$.

Returning to the question why in 1962–1973 the income distribution has not changed so much as the figures of Table 7.II suggest, two points seem to be relevant. One is that only some recent student generations have doubled in comparison to the composition of the labour force; it will take some decades before the composition of the entire labour force will be as indicated in Table 7.II. In addition, there may also have been changes on the side of demand for qualified manpower, showing up as possible changes in the parameters of the production function. In fact, these questions have already been dealt with in Chapter 6.

7.6. Optimality of income distribution: some more details

In Section 7.5 we applied the method proposed to define optimal income distribution to the crude five-compartment material for the Netherlands. The somewhat more detailed data presented in Chapter 4 for the Netherlands and for some American states enable us to go into some more detail by applying the same method to the larger number of groups considered there – 21 for the Netherlands and about 15 for each of the American states considered.

For the utility function proposed in Chapter 4, optimality implies that, according to equation (7.30), utilities of the groups considered *must be equal*. Using the notation of Chapter 4, where s characterized jobs by indicating the years of schooling needed in multiples of 3 years and v was education actually completed in the same units, Table 7.VI shows, alongside the actual incomes x after tax, the optimal values in parentheses calculated with the aid of the numerical specification,

$$x = +0.45s + 0.32(s - v)^2 + 5.7. \qquad (7.35)$$

The constant has been chosen so as to obtain the average labour income after tax for the two corresponding combinations $(s = 2, v = 3)$ and $(s = v = 2)$ as it actually was in 1962.

Table 7.VI
Actual and optimal income distribution under the assumption set out in text (optimal in parentheses); 1962, in thousands of Dfl.

s	v				
	2	3	4	5	6
6	.	.	14.0 (9.7)	14.0 (8.7)	14.0 (8.4)
5	.	11.3 (9.2)	11.3 (8.3)	11.3 (8.0)	11.3 (8.3)
4	8.3 (8.8)	8.3 (7.8)	8.3 (7.5)	8.3 (7.8)	8.3 (8.8)
3	9.9 (7.4)	10.2 (7.1)	10.5 (7.4)	10.8 (7.2)	.
2[a]	4.9 (6.6)	7.7 (6.9)	.	.	.

[a] Weighted average of two groups for $v = 2$ mentioned in Table 7.I.

The reader should be reminded that our assumptions in Chapter 4 are that v and W constitute parameters in the strict sense, hence cannot be changed by some learning process. To the extent that v or W or both can be obtained by efforts constituting a sacrifice, our formula (7.35) should obtain terms in v and W or both, expressing the corresponding sacrifices. These terms cannot surpass the additional scarcity incomes at present enjoyed by those endowed with higher values of v or W. If v and W are parameters in the strict sense, then the optimal income distribution can be reached by measures counteracting the scarcity incomes, without killing the stimuli for the better endowed individuals. This problem will be taken up in further detail in Chapter 8.

For the state of Illinois we found, in the notation used in Section 4.5, the utility function's argument to be $x = -0.156h - 0.06(h - h')^2$; and equality of utility would therefore mean that this expression is the same for all groups considered. Its value was chosen equal to the value for the most numerous group, represented by $h = 6$ and $h' = 8$, which happens to be a group near the median as well. Accordingly optimal incomes were estimated with the aid of (7.36),

$$x = 0.156h + 0.06(h - h')^2 + 3.4. \tag{7.36}$$

Table 7.VII

Actual and (in parentheses) optimal income for groups with different occupations h and education h'; Illinois, 1959, in thousands of US $.

h	h'							
	0	3	6	8	10	12	14	18
0	3.1 (3.4)	3.3 (3.9)						
3		3.4 (3.9)	3.7 (4.4)					
6			4.2 (4.3)	4.6 (4.6)				
8				4.6 (4.7)	5.1 (4.9)			
10					5.7 (5.0)	6.2 (5.2)		
12						6.7 (5.3)		
14						7.2 (5.8)	7.8 (5.6)	
18							8.4 (7.1)	9.5 (6.2)

Table 7.VII shows the actual and (in parentheses) the optimal incomes for all groups, assuming the very provisional conditions specified.

The interesting feature of both Table 7.VI and Table 7.VII is the reduction in inequality they require in order to arrive at an optimal income distribution as here estimated. The difference between highest and lowest incomes after taxes for the groups considered should be reduced by 66 per cent for the Netherlands in 1962 and by 56 per cent for Illinois in 1959.

In Table 7.VIII some more information on the same subject is given in a more summarized form for the other American states discussed (cf. Section 4.6).

Table 7.VIII

Actual and optimal income differences for labour with different schooling, derived from the first attempt to measure utility functions; 1959, in thousands of US $.

State	Differences between incomes of labour without schooling and			
	(I) Labour with 18 years schooling		(II) Labour with 12 years schooling	
	Actual	Optimal	Actual	Optimal
Cal	6.3	4.4 (2.2)	3.4	2.9 (1.4)
Ill	6.4	2.8 (2.7)	3.6	1.8 (1.8)
NY	6.1	4.5 (2.2)	3.2	3.0 (1.5)
Mich	7.9	3.1 (2.0)	3.4	2.1 (1.3)
SoCa	5.7	1.7 (1.7)	2.9	1.1 (1.2)
Tex	6.0	1.9 (2.1)	3.4	1.3 (1.4)
Wis	5.8	1.9 (1.8)	2.9	1.3 (1.2)

Optimal figures have been estimated with the aid of first regression values of c_0 (Table 4.VII) from the quadratic tension method and (in parentheses) values of c_0 obtained from the linear tension method. They apply to groups for which $h = h'$ (that is, on the diagonal in Table 7.VII).

8

Equitable income distribution

8.1. Difficulties around the concept of justice or equity

For centuries mankind has been interested in justice or equity
in socio-economic affairs. As an illustration we only need to
quote the mediaeval discussion of the concept of *iustum
pretium*, the equitable price, not only for commodities but also
for the borrowing of capital. Economists generally adhere to
the opinion that the definition of justice is not part of their
science, but rather of ethics, morals or the philosophy of law.
Yet the problem cannot be solved either by representatives of
these disciplines and until quite recently not much of a useful
answer has come from them. What answers have been given,
even by respectable scholars such as Perelman [51], hardly
surpass the self-evident – justice requires equal treatment of
equals. What has to be done with unequals remained in the
dark. This state of affairs is understandable, however, since the
problem of defining justice or equity cannot be solved without
knowledge about the consequences of changing the economy
on the basis of some equity concept. And the search for these
consequences does belong to the realm of economic science.
Clearly, then, the problem is interdisciplinary and either
requires co-operation between economists and moralists
or study by one person of two disciplines. Lately some
remarkable work has been published by Rawls [55] and by
Roscam Abbing [57]. This chapter attempts to make another
contribution, directed more particularly at what seems to be
measurable at this time. We must remain aware of the tentative
and provisional nature of what can be done in the present state

of the debate and with the limited knowledge obtained by measurements that we have of the relevant aspects.

It seems appropriate, though, to remain aware of the long and deep-digging history of the search for justice or equity and even *equality*. That last word has been used in such solemn declarations as those by theologians about 'equality before God', by lawyers about 'equality in court' and by politicians about 'equal voting rights'. The last reflects the primitive way in which at present most Western societies – and since a relatively short span of time only – make their collective decisions.

It also seems appropriate to put on record that because of a process of rapid development of all possible types of measurement we are increasingly well-informed about the many ways in which human beings are *unequal*. In crude experiments unequal physical strength of different individuals of a same species of animal is established periodically and used in violent processes of selection to determine the hierarchy and leadership in collective action. More refined measurements and studies of the inequalities measured are presented in the work of early statisticians such as Quetelet [53] and have since expanded over a real labyrinth of physical and psychical properties of, among other animals, man. *Physical measurements* have been extended beyond well-known measures needed for apparel or for beauty, to all sorts of details of the body, among them skull features. *Psychical measurements* probably found their earliest representatives in school marks, later followed by IQ 'and all that', whereas relatively recent surveys have dealt with occupational status. Alongside direct measurement of the capabilities of individuals an enormous arsenal of standards has been created in what is known as *job evaluation*. Strictly speaking this technique measures *job requirements*, but implicitly each appointment of an individual to a particular job also measures the person involved. An increasing number of types of examinations in the form of comparisons among participants add to the huge volume of information now available but hardly used for our purpose.

In the face of this state of affairs this study proposes to accept inequality of individuals in a large number of respects, but only *when measured*. This seems a scientifically sound attitude. We propose to combine this scientific contribution with an *ethical postulate* that despite all inequalities a hard core of 'fundamental equality' remains as has always been felt by religious and political idealists referred to above. A more down-to-earth interpretation of this 'fundamental equality' or 'equivalence' is also conceivable: the fact that each human being is a member of the human race in contradistinction to other living beings. What is added in this study is a concrete *mathematical* expression, introduced in Chapter 4, of 'fundamental equality' or 'equivalence' by postulating that the utility functions of all human beings have the same mathematical shape and the same coefficients. This postulate enables us to make a primitive start at measuring utility.

8.2. Evolution of the economist's concept of equity

The present attitude of agnosticism vis-à-vis a definition of equity or justice which is also preferred by most economists was preceded by a period in which many economists whom we in Europe today call liberalist – or Manchester liberals – did have a definition of justice. Justice was considered to consist of the equality between an individual's *income received* from society and his *contribution* to society by making available part of the production factors he owned. The definition is typically individualistic in that it deals with the relationship of each individual to society as an abstract entity and does not compare individuals to each other, at least not directly.

In increasing numbers members of our society are doubting this interpretation of what we feel when we speak about justice or equity. Two implications of a new concept of justice stand out. One is that the factors 'nature' (or 'land') and capital can be 'owned' and that the justice of this *ownership* is debatable. The other implication is that personal capability, although an intrinsic part of a personality, is a gift of God or Nature –

different formulations are possible here – and its distribution among individuals is *not necessarily equitable* either. While two elements of doubt lead us to deny the appropriateness of the definition quoted, they do not automatically provide us with a new concept.

Our positive suggestion consists of adhering to the definition that equity stands for *equal welfare for all individuals*. For economists welfare is identical to utility in its broadest sense and is also identical to happiness in a restricted sense. The happiness meant might be indicated as '*social* happiness', that is happiness as far as it is dependent on social variables and parameters, or variables and parameters as far as they are relevant for the individual's *role in society*. It excludes such entirely personal elements as friendship, love, or religion; and there are more. The frontier between personal and social may be a matter for debate and may also shift over time. Clearly we are up against a realm of analysis hardly opened up yet.

From the definition proposed it is clear that it is *unacceptable* to those who deny the measurability of utility. In the debate on measurability our point of view is that the only statement that can be reasonably made in this controversy is that so far utility has not been measured *with great precision*. To us it seems unacceptable to maintain that utility *cannot* be measured. It is an essential ingredient of scientific activity to try to work with measured concepts, since measurement only can show a possible incompatibility between a theory and reality. For a long time now political and family decisions have been made which in fact are based on a vague and intuitive way of measuring welfare, of making comparisons between the welfare of different groups or persons. Both Parliament and individual households currently make such decisions. In Parliament and sometimes in other institutions the element of arbitrariness in these vague and intuitive decisions is reduced by the system of *voting*, comparable to checking measurements of a more scientific character by repeating measurements. In many sciences we observe the evolution of measurement from a vague and crude classification ranking and finally to cardinal

_ measurement as the most perfect method of measurement. While in the beginning measurement may be done in a somewhat arbitrary way, further research may later lead to giving more background to the method chosen and to distinguishing between various alternative methods for different problems. Thus, heat was originally considered a 'feeling' with no possibilities for being measured; later the thermometer was introduced as an instrument of measurement. Subsequently physicists began to make a distinction between the 'degree' of heat, called *temperature*, and the quantity of heat, one of the forms of the more general concept of *energy*. The thermometer can be said to have been based on the experience that most substances expand proportionally and that, in a way, these substances, by 'majority vote', tell us what temperature is. Only a majority indeed and not unanimity, since there are a number of circumstances under which a given substance behaves differently, for instance at its melting or its boiling point.

Our method of measuring welfare or utility has been set out in Chapter 4 and some use of it has been made in Chapter 7, where a *social* welfare function was introduced, equal to the unweighted sum of individual (or household) welfare. With its help a precise meaning could be given to social optimality. In this section an additional attempt has been made to give a more precise meaning to the concept of justice or equity.

8.3. Implications of proposed definition; equity and optimality

A few simple implications of the proposed definition of equity may illustrate its character, especially by informing us about what equity is not. It was observed already that equity cannot mean equality, since in many respects individual members of a community decidedly are not equal and cannot be made equal.

In addition it can be easily seen that equity does *not* imply *equality of income*. This would only follow under a number of additional assumptions which are not warranted at all. A sufficient assumption would be that welfare only depends on income. In that case equality of welfare implies equality of income. Since welfare, even in the simple illustrative case used in this study, depends also on such variables as occupation chosen, or such parameters as number of years of schooling, equality of welfare will not, in a general way, imply equality of income. Similarly, incomes of *households of different size* will not have to be equal in order to attain an equitable income distribution. It is conceivable to regulate other variables, such as working hours, with the purpose of letting equality of incomes coincide with equity, but it is not a necessary but rather an arbitrary regulation.

Finally a comparison between *equity and optimality* seems helpful for a clear understanding of both concepts. Optimality of a socio-economic state of affairs means that social welfare has been maximized under a set of restrictions imposed by the environment of nature and natural laws. With the choice made in this book for the definition of social welfare, discrimination has been avoided by giving equal weights to all individuals or all individual households. Yet the maximum of social welfare need not imply equal welfare for all. It so happens that in the particular model used in Chapter 7 optimality does imply equality of welfare for all. This is due to some particularly symmetrical properties of our model. More precisely, equations (7.24) through (7.29) express this coincidence of optimality and equity and it is easy to see that this need not apply for more complicated utility functions. Thus, if utility were, for an individual (h, h'),

$$\omega_{hh'} = f\{x_{hh'}(1 + c_3 h) - c_0 h + c_1 h' - \tfrac{1}{2} c_2 (h - h')^2\},$$

$$(8.1)$$

optimalization of total welfare would require, instead of (7.24), etc.,

$$f'\{\ \}(1 + c_3 h) + \tau = 0, \tag{8.2}$$

or equality of $f'\{\ \}(1 + c_3 h)$ which does not imply equality of all $\omega_{hh'}$.

Of course we can pose *another problem*, namely the maximization of social welfare subject to the *constraint of equity*.

Generally this will be a solvable problem, but a more complicated one; and as a rule the solution will constitute a lower value of social welfare – every additional restriction will lead to lower social welfare in the optimum position. Generally speaking, with all $\omega_{hh'}$ equal, the $\partial\omega_{hh'}/\partial x_{hh'}$ will no longer be equal, since optimum conditions (7.24) through (7.29) will now become considerably more complicated.

Our conclusion is that equity and optimality are concepts of a different kind, that optimality need not imply equity, but that equity and optimality can be combined at the expense of some social welfare. This sacrifice happens to be zero in our special case.

Some *final remarks* are needed about the *institutional implications* of our definition of an equitable income distribution. In fact we should repeat the question posed in paragraph 7.7 with regard to optimality: Is equity feasible and, if not, can we indicate the institutions needed to attain feasibility? As an answer we must first repeat that our models are highly simplified and that a distinction must be made between these models and more complicated ones. In our models the only institutions explicitly involved are factor markets and educational, research, and tax institutions. The limitations which have shown to be possible for the realization of equity are similar to the ones discussed with respect to optimality. As far as markets are concerned *monopolies of high income groups* cannot be accepted. *Educational* limitations may be either *natural*, if an insufficient number of individuals can absorb higher education or training, or *institutional*, if an insufficient access to education exists. Since in our model optimality and equity coincide, Table 7.V illustrates the orders of magnitude involved. At the level of technology existing in 1962 six to seven per cent of the active population should be able to absorb higher education and this is about double the percentage that had such an education in 1960. If we may assume that higher education absorption is proportional to university education absorption, Table 6.VI suggests that before 1980 the 6 to 7 per cent level will be reached. *Techno-*

logical development as it has advanced so far will, however, continue to increase the demand for more people with higher education. If the ratio of the income of university graduates to the income of all labour is to be kept constant, the percentage of academically trained people around 1990 must be at least 40 per cent higher than around 1975: this figure can be derived from the last two columns of Table 6.V. In this respect Passenier's figures (Table 6.VI) are encouraging. But a time may come when this problem becomes more difficult. This depends also on the possibilities of *reorienting research* in the direction so that fewer highly trained individuals are required for the years beyond the year 2000 than the present trend implies.

As for the *tax system*, we already emphasized the possible limitations of our present system. While the optimum does require, in generalized models, the lump-sum tax system already discussed in Section 7.7, we can repeat that with our simplified model even the rather progressive tax studied in case B⁗ of Table 7.III does not satisfy the conditions for income after tax needed according to Table 7.V. Perhaps much higher taxes on capital income could produce the necessary redistribution and this would constitute an institutional change in the direction of *traditional socialist* policies.

Only further refinement of utility measurement will be able to give us information about whether equity meets stronger or weaker limitations than optimal income distribution. Without specifying and testing such more complicated utility functions as mentioned above we cannot make more precise statements.

8.4. Effects of neglected factors

Clearly the very simple illustrative examples of how to estimate welfare functions need many corrections. When applied to individuals or individual households, such parameters as age or the number of members of households can be easily introduced, as has been shown by Van Praag [79]. At the same time, there is hardly any need to introduce them for groups of approximately the same age distribution or household size distribution. The differences in the coefficients found for the Netherlands and for the states of the USA, however, point out the necessity of finding parameters characterizing different ethnic groups. Thus, differences in the coefficient c_0 signify different relative valuations of money (that is, consumption) with regard to additional efforts. Similarly, differences in c_2 may be interpreted as differences in the relative valuation of money and 'doing work below or above one's capabilities'. We already formulated some alternative assumptions concerning these latter two differences in Section 4.6.

On some of the additional parameters or variables some more information is already available. Thus, the possible difference in *working hours* between wage and salary earners in the Netherlands appears to be negligible, according to a recent inquiry by the Free University of Amsterdam. Also the inquiries by Van Praag and collaborators [79, 80] mentioned earlier contain additional information on the differences between the *utility functions* for families in which the *wife works* and for families in which the *wife doesn't work*. The additional influence of *working experience* can also be read from our equation (3.12).

Evidently a vast programme of further research is called for. The present study is meant to make a start for some of this research, but its results can only be considered first attempts.

9

Income distribution policies

9.1. Definition; objectives

We will define as income distribution policies all intervention into the process of income formation with the general objective of changing income distribution. Intervention need not restrict itself to the income formation process proper, that is the forces of demand for and supply of labour of different types or other production factors such as capital. This type of intervention may be called *direct* intervention; well-known examples are the imposition of *minimum wages*, the limitation of *dividends* and so on. Such policies, if not based on a careful analysis of the operation of the markets concerned, may unexpectedly disrupt market equilibrium, possibly even to the disadvantage of those whom the authorities want to assist. A broader spectrum of policies are those which have an impact on the forces 'behind' the markets concerned; in German they are known as '*marktkonform*'. We will call them *indirect* policies. Their advantage is that they do not disrupt but rather shift the equilibrium, although the differences with direct policies are not as sharp as some authors have suggested. In one way or another income distribution policies are meant to change the free market order or *laissez-faire*, exactly because the outcome of such a completely free system is considered to be ethically unacceptable. This they have in common with a long list of modern public interferences, from the prohibition of child labour to the imposition of ecological standards.

Among indirect income distribution policies, intervention by educational, tax, social security, and technological research policies will be discussed, corresponding with our discussions in preceding chapters. While tax and social security policies have been applied for a long time in order to influence income distribution, so far educational and research policies have usually been pursued with other main objectives in mind. But we have found that their impact on income distribution might be of some importance.

While the general objective of income distribution policies may be said to be to reduce income differences, there are also other objectives; at present, for instance, to *reduce inflation* or price rises. Moreover, the degree of reduction in income inequalities aimed at is a matter of lively discussion. Several public opinion inquiries have confirmed more precisely the well-known fact that opinions on the present income distribution and on the direction in which it should be changed widely vary. It is precisely with this phenomenon in mind that in this study we have tried to give some more precise content to such concepts as optimal and equitable income distribution. It should be kept in mind, however, that our attempts have also confirmed that a definition of either of these concepts does not imply that the means exist to attain such distributions.

In the setup of this book the present chapter is intended to somewhat fill the gaps between the crude framework constructed in the preceding chapters and the *large number of details* which characterize practical income distribution policies. It is not our intention to add new points of view here but rather to remind the reader of the many gaps. In doing so we will draw heavily on what other authors, scientists as well as men and women of practical experience, have said or written. Our great debt to these authors will be clear to the reader on many occasions. If we do not attempt to quote many of these other authors it is because the setup of this book would not permit an equilibrated documentation of this kind.

9.2. Survey of means used in present income distribution policies

As already stated, a large number of policies, pursued by different institutions, are currently directed at the objective of attaining an income distribution more in accordance with what present-day public opinion considers desirable. In this section a quick survey will be given, in a more or less chronological order of the initiation of these activities. Our survey will cover a time span of more than a century, starting in the first half of the nineteenth century, but touching only upon the most important institutions and policies.

Trade unions were the first among the more important institutions which considered it their task to improve living conditions of their members with the aid of what the economist would call oligopolistic activities. Even though, according to some production functions, such activities cannot raise the portion of national product distributed to workers as a group, they may have had other types of impact on society, such as reducing traditional inertia and speeding up the formation of capital and technological development. According to other production functions, trade unions can indeed raise the workers' share in national income.

Social legislation is a second large complex of policies, usually administered by public or semi-public bodies, directed at helping the socially weak. A distinction can be made between social *insurance* and social *assistance*, but the dividing line is not sharp. Generally there has been a movement from individual insurance principles towards instantaneous redistribution. Both systems are characterized by the collection of contributions and the distribution of benefits. The pure insurance institutions are in addition the owners of a capital and as a consequence have a second source of income, interest on accumulated capital. The pure redistribution institutions aim at an annual balance between contributions levied and benefits paid out. There is also a good deal of variation with regard to eligibility for participation in an institution. Many of the earlier institutions of social security were set up for *employees* only or even for *state employees.*

They contributed little if anything to general social issues. The bulk of the later social security institutions were created for *wage earners* in manufacturing industry and services and were not accessible to agricultural workers or domestic workers. Still later their coverage was also extended to these groups.

The redistribution they effectuated was one *among* workers rather than between workers and the middle and upper classes. Deleeck [19] feels this is to a large extent still true in Belgium. Probably this is true to a large extent also in France and other Latin countries.

After the worst inequalities had been reduced, a number of social institutions were also made accessible to *small independents;* separate provisions were made for agriculture. Some of the latter hardly reduced inequality among agriculturists. This is true when the measures aimed at raising prices of agricultural products, as those taken during the Great Depression and in protective countries.

In the last few decades social provisions were organized benefiting *all citizens* in difficult circumstances, such as illness, or old age.

The subjects covered by social security are not exactly the same in all countries, but there is a good deal of similarity. Starting with provisions for victims of *accidents* or *professional diseases,* gradually such subjects as *unemployment, illness, hospitalization* or *old age,* were covered and provisions for *large families, widows* and *orphans* were introduced. Even if about the same type of measures have been taken, the quantitative extent of the benefits and hence of the necessary contributions sometimes differ considerably among countries. Two main elements determine the level of social provisions: the country's average income and its general philosophy or, in other words, its political tendencies. Thus, the United States introduced social security on a larger scale only during the Great Depression, when the prevailing *laissez-faire* philosophy went through a severe confidence crisis; in Western Europe most countries had introduced them long before.

Taxes have been used as instruments of redistribution since the beginning of the twentieth century; we begin with *direct* taxes, such as taxes on income, wealth and wealth increases, which because of their progressive character imply that relatively larger contributions were required from the well-to-do for financing the public sector. While for a long time *indirect* taxes were more or less proportional to expenditure and hence, by and large, to income, gradually they have been made progressive by the exemption of first *necessities* and the additional taxing of *luxuries*.

The social role of taxation became more outspoken when, step by step, the volume of *services* rendered to the general public *below cost* was extended. This applies especially to education, which was increasingly financed by public authorities and, moreover, expanded very quickly during the last century. Today it also applies to rail transport and, in some countries, to medical services.

While the largest volume of transfers made as a consequence of the policies summed up can be described as indirect income distribution policies, on a number of occasions governments have also applied *direct policies* as defined in Section 9.1. During the Great Depression, during both world wars, after these wars and in the last decade both *wages* and *prices* have been the subject of government interference, usually in consultation with the large organizations of the employees and employers concerned. Minimum wages, whether in particular branches of activity or in general, are one example. Wage stops for a limited period constitute another case. Prices of first necessities are subject to government control in several countries; alternatively, price increases need the authorities' permission. Inversely, as a means of protecting some groups of small producers in agriculture, small-scale industry, and retail trade, minimum prices for their products are currently being fixed.

In some countries, which were under foreign occupation

during World War II, for quite some time after that war a system of *co-operation between government and the organizations of employees and employers* was in successful operation with the aim of maintaining some sort of temporary social harmony in order to speed up the economy's reconstruction from war damage. The Netherlands are probably the best-known case, but France and Norway knew similar forms of co-operation. In Holland and Norway two background factors were operative which might be revived in the future, provided the appropriate formulation of the 'common interest' can be found. One was a feeling of solidarity against outside forces; the other was an increased influence of economic science as a platform of rational discussion. For the last fifteen years these factors have weakened and the situation considered more normal in most countries has returned. In fact, the situation has become even more than before, one of *confrontation* of group and class interests.

9.3. Generalized inflation

Until around 1960 inflation was considered to be an abnormal phenomenon which had occurred in a number of developed countries as a particularly post-war problem and in a few developing countries, mainly Brazil and Chile, as a 'structural' problem. The famous case in developed countries was the *German* inflation of 1921–1923, described as 'galloping inflation', due to a particular combination of factors such as the imposition by the Allied powers of a war indemnity and a transition of power to a democratic socialist government anxious to meet the wishes of the workers. With the aid of a big stabilization loan and the return to normal financial policies the German government succeeded in the operation of price stabilization after the old mark had been depreciated to one-billionth (in the European sense of 10^{-12}) of its 1913 value. Even more serious depreciations occurred in Hungary, but they have attracted less attention. More moderate depreciations reduced the Belgian, French and Italian currencies, leaving these currencies around 1960 at about one-seventh, one-fiftieth and one-eightieth of their 1913 gold parities. As a consequence of the Great Depression the US dollar was devalued in 1933 and the British pound in 1931. Several smaller changes, sometimes revaluations, took place after World War II, among other countries in Germany, Switzerland and the Netherlands.

The long-lasting inflations and corresponding depreciations and devaluations in *Brazil* and *Chile* were the most spectacular examples in a number of developing countries after 1945, especially in Latin America but also elsewhere. The phenomena in Latin America were the source of a scientific discussion between two 'schools' known as the *monetarist* and the *structural* school. The monetarist school recommended, as the only real remedy to the continual price rises (often of about fifty per cent per annum), the adaptation of national expenditures to national income. It can be easily shown that such an adaptation implies equilibrium in the current items of the balance of payments. The monetarists understood that the main obstacle is this *'financial discipline'* which is difficult to live up to for countries with 'soft governments' which are desirous of investing large amounts in objects of development such as infrastructure or also state industries. The structuralists tried to point out that some features of the countries' structure constitute the obstacle to a healthier policy. In this author's opinion the real structural difficulty in carrying out the monetarists' counsel consists of the existence of so-called *'non-tradables'*, that is, goods which cannot enter into international trade. Examples are buildings, roads, a large number of services and often electricity, as long as there are no interconnected networks. The adaptation of national expenditure to national income, as recommended by the monetarists, also implies a substantial reduction in the demand for non-tradables and hence a reduction in national income. While a reduction in internal demand for tradables creates an exportable surplus, this is not true for a reduction in the demand for non-tradables. The substantial reduction in national product and income implied by the monetarists' recommendation is the real stumbling block. Instead, a policy mix should have been recommended, including not only the adaptation of national expenditure to national income, but also a production-increasing device to compensate for the loss of income otherwise incurred: for instance, an expansion of the production capacity of exportables or import substitution of tradables [71].

An important further example of galloping inflation in a developing country is found in *Indonesia* around 1965. Here an outright lack of understanding of economic problems by President Sukarno, the country's cultural and political leader during its struggle for independence, was at the root of developments. Sukarno's merits in other fields are great enough to permit us to bluntly state this fact. The present government has succeeded in overcoming the worst part of inflation.

After 1960 developed countries got increasingly involved in a process of '*creeping inflation*', especially Western European developed countries. For some time the United States stayed out, whereas Japan, besides experiencing the most spectacular rate of real growth – some ten per cent per annum for about two decades – suffered from a process of worse inflation. Western Europe's creeping inflation was felt to be an almost unavoidable side-effect of its full-employment policy, which was successful for quite some time: in most countries the rate of unemployment stayed far below Beveridge's three per cent norm. The bargaining position of trade unions was automatically strengthened by this policy, which was not pursued in the United States and couldn't be applied yet in Japan with at that time a rural labour reserve.

Around 1970 the creeping inflation increased in momentum and at the moment of writing amounted to an annual ten per cent price increase. In reaching this level the problem of inflation has become an *important social problem* which only countries with a centrally planned economy have been able to keep under control. It represents an urgent challenge to the democratic Western countries and deserves some further analysis. Even some degree of undesirable unemployment, say of over three per cent, has not yet halted the rise in prices and wages and has led instead to situations known as 'stagflation' – stagnation with inflation. While definitely part of the problem resides, as before, in a lack of financial discipline, another and maybe the larger component is an aspect of income distribution, even of labour income distribution. We will consider first this latter aspect and turn to the distribution of wealth in Section 9.4.

The general point to be made first is that the present ten per cent per annum price rises can no longer be considered to be an advantage to *the masses*. One or two per cent rises have sometimes been defended as an element of 'lubricating oil' in the economy, helpful to new ventures and hence to the maintenance of employment. At the ten per cent level the situation can be better characterized as one in which all sorts of speculation absorb an indefensible portion of national product to the detriment of all those who make really productive contributions. If the well-known phrase 'getting richer while asleep' applies to clever capital owners, then it applies with fuller justification to the automatic enrichment of all holders of physical capital, whether they do or don't make an effort to intelligently use that physical capital.

The next point to be made is that present-day inflation is to a considerable extent '*cost-push*' inflation, distinct from 'demand-pull' inflation; which was already dealt with, in other words, when the monetary aspect was mentioned. Cost-push inflation becomes important when, as is true, most social groups simultaneously claim a larger piece of the pie of national product: workers, employees, farmers and most other entrepreneurs, all of them in turn. In nominal terms they ask for increases in their shares which add up to more than the real annual increase in production and increasingly more. Most of these groups are unaware of the consequence: that the price rises they cause by this unco-ordinated *hunt for more* decreases their relative shares to the advantage of speculators.

The only sensible way out of this maelstrom is an attempt

to agree on some more objective yardstick for the future distribution. Of course, such a yardstick – accepted by a considerable majority of the citizens – may not be found. In order to facilitate an agreement on this subject, two elements seem to be useful. One is an awareness of the history of income distribution and its causes. The other is an ethical principle for the choices open to us. This study attempts to contribute to both elements; the emphasis must be on 'contribute' since the eventual agreement, if one can be attained, will have to rest on contributions by many students of the problem.

As for the mechanism of the history of income distribution, it seems useful to stress the almost monotonous *reduction in inequality*, attained partly through the mechanism of demand and supply. With regard to the ethical principle, a *more precise definition of equity* may be of some help. Of some help only, since the definition of equity does not yet warrant, as we saw, its materialization. It is only within the limits set by the policy instruments at our disposal that equity – when adhered to in the process of a dialogue – can be attained. Hence the importance of extending the arsenal of policy instruments.

The *type of agreement* conceivable in the present circumstances seems to this author to be a long-term (say, a five-year or ten-year) agreement on the increase in the portion of national product allocated to the lowest income groups. Such an agreement, once accepted, should be the framework of socio-economic planning. It should be accompanied by the acceptance, by parliament, of a solid financial discipline. A better financial discipline will be furthered by an intensified *integration*, first of all, of the European Community. National parliaments can be put under some pressure by the argument that international agreements are involved. But then the agreements should indeed be concluded, evidently a difficult thing for British and French politicians to accept.

In addition, the search for better instruments of income distribution policies should be intensified. Section 9.5 will deal with this subject. First the element of the distribution of wealth will be briefly discussed.

9.4. The distribution of wealth

Part of the income distribution clearly depends on the distribution of wealth, not only because unearned income derives from wealth, but also because wealth constitutes a reserve for its owner and so enhances his manoeuvring possibilities. This has been understood ever since Marx, and an enormous literature exists on the various alternative ways in which the impact of wealth on income and power distribution can be reduced. There is no point in even trying to summarize this literature. This author does not adhere to the theory that *complete socialization* is the best way of dealing with even productive wealth and that partial solutions are bound to fail. As support of this view it may be stated that, although wealth distribution is more uneven than income distribution, it is also becoming less unequal fairly quickly, as shown by Atkinson [1]. Partly as a consequence of the expansion of social security institutions and, for another part, of the expansion of private insurance companies, an increasing part of total wealth belongs to lower income groups. Trade unions are preparing schemes for workers' participation in enterprise capital and some of these are likely to come into operation.

A well-known difficulty of getting certain types of financial manipulations under control is the shiftability of unearned income into capital gains in order to profit from the low tax rate on the latter (or even the absence of such a tax). Kaldor's proposal [35] on how to administer an expenditure rather than an income tax seems to be important especially for developed countries and has had less support than it deserves.

While this author views further rises in death duties favourably and sees their link with the receiver's rather than with the donor's wealth, he has nothing to add to the debate on this topic.

9.5. Further proposals on income distribution policies derived from the present study

Alongside the policies described in the preceding sections of this chapter, a few more can be suggested on the basis of our present study.

(i) *Educational policies* deserve to be programmed not only with a view to improving education in the widest sense, but also in order to influence income distribution. In most of our results, perhaps clearest in Chapter 6, the equalizing consequences of extended education are reflected. Since the heart of the matter is to approach, as much as possible, equality between the demand for and the supply of the manifold types of labour, our recommendation is not simply a quantitative one, but requires many qualitative changes in education as well. Part of these may be approached from the demand side, as reflected in job evaluation, but an interdependence and a mutual impact of cultural elements on both the demand and the supply side may considerably enrich this complex of policies.

(ii) In order to create more clarity on the *aims* of income distribution policies, the elaboration of our concepts of welfare, is strongly recommended. A vast programme of further research and of exchange of ideas on these subjects seems to be called for and can be easily formulated.

(iii) Since *technological development* also affects the demand for various types of labour and needs a fresh look for reasons of environmental policies, a broad discussion of priorities in technological research looks promising also for reasons of income distribution. Now that the awareness of the multiple freedoms of choice in this field has grown considerably, the income distribution aspect of these choices should also be kept in mind.

(iv) As shown by simple examples in Chapter 7 and as is well known from welfare economics, a search for entirely different tax types, closer to *lump-sum taxes* and possibly based on human capabilities rather than on the results of their use, is imperative. Most important in this field clearly is the development of *psychotechnical testing*, the contribution of which is vital, whether negative or positive.

10

Summary and conclusions

10.1. Main contributions of present study

In the preceding chapters an attempt has been made to integrate some of the main economic theories on the distribution of incomes in Western developed countries. By *economic* theories I mean theories which specify the variables used, in contradistinction to what could be called *stochastic* theories, where the mechanism of income formation is described by the specification of the variables' statistical behaviour, but the latters' nature is not specified. Of course the existence of random components is not denied; every time a correlation coefficient below 1 is obtained they are implied. It is, however, the author's conviction that a stochastic theory constitutes an intermediate product of theorizing only and has to be followed by attempts to specify the most important stochastic components.

The main economic theories of income distribution so far presented emphasize somewhat either the supply or the demand side. This book joins those authors who have already attempted to give a place to both sides.

The studies presented here try to avoid duplication of the existing literature, although this is never completely possible – every scholar builds on what his predecessors have done and rightly so. The attempt to *avoid duplication* is the best excuse for the slight attention given to income from *capital;* a second argument being that incomes after taxes contain only a small portion from capital and that increasingly income-after-tax differences are due to differences in *human* capital.

This is much less true for developing countries. These have only been mentioned on a few occasions and as a contrast. It is the author's hope that scholars and politicians from developing countries may in the present study find something of interest for their future policies.

The book has been kept simple; first of all because it would have been beyond the author's power to make it complicated, but also because complicated models often prevent the reader from seeing the forest because of the large number of trees. Finally simplicity is imposed by the lack of generally accessible statistical data.

In contradistinction to the book's simplicity the author claims some degree of depth in two respects. First, some sort of a complete semi-macro model for the Netherlands has been presented in Chapter 7, enabling us to 'explain' some features of quantitative income distribution and to demonstrate variation and optimization exercises. And secondly, an unorthodox attempt has been made to work with 'measured utility (or welfare)'. No doubt the greatest controversy about this book will concentrate on this issue. It would not be difficult, even for this author, to write a convincing and killing critique and many such reviews will be written. Constructive criticism will be more valuable, however, and must consist of alternative approaches. The author is happy to know that some such alternatives will be forthcoming.

In the complete model also a production function with five types of labour has been used. Ignoring the trends of the profession a function was chosen with some Cobb–Douglas features, mainly again for simplicity's sake. The author has tried to justify his choice with the aid of a number of elasticity estimates given in Chapter 5.

10.2. Demand and supply method

As already observed, this study constitutes an attempt to integrate income distribution theories mainly emphasizing the *supply* of types of labour with those mainly emphasizing the *demand* for them. Authors such as Freeman and Ullman have already made such attempts, but important schools of thought such as the human capital school and the education planning school have somewhat overemphasized supply or demand, respectively. For long-run studies the approach chosen here seems more satisfactory, as illustrated by Chapter 6, dealing with changes during the period 1900–1990 for the United States and the Netherlands.

The particular advantages of a combined demand and supply approach are the following. Such a theory reminds us, to begin with, of the fact that for income equalization *equal capabilities of all individuals are not required*, but rather equality of the demand for and the supply of the various different types of production factors, in particular labour. Secondly, a demand–supply theory reminds us that *important shifts* in income ratios are natural in contradistinction to the maintenance, preferred by the privileged, of historical ratios. Thirdly, a demand–supply theory helps us find the factors (demand and supply factors, as defined in Chapter 3) *behind* the labour market, some of which may be susceptible to manipulation, in order to change income distribution. This is not only true for taxes, but also for education and for technological development (see Chapter 6).

Apart from such considerations it is quite natural for an economist to think in terms of demand and supply. It should be added that such an ordering of our thoughts is much more flexible than some representatives of other social sciences (law, sociology) think and that many of the so-called *non-economic* factors determining income distribution can be easily subsumed under the concepts of demand and supply. Thus, such restrictive forces as the *caste* system of India, can be said to co-determine the supply of some types of labour. The same applies in Western countries to the prejudices against *manual* (blue-collar) work as distinct from white-collar work.

10.3. Numerical results obtained

The various chapters of this book contain a succession of studies which at the same time constitute an evolution in the author's thinking. Up to a point they present results which can be seen as tests of theories presented by others; but it has to be kept in mind that the theories used in the early chapters, especially Chapters 2 and 3, are less sophisticated than those used in the later chapters, mainly Chapters 4 to 7 inclusive. Thus, in Chapter 3 the technological level was considered a constant, an assumption abandoned in Chapters 6 and 7.

Chapter 2 constitutes a simple collection of *figures* referring to different periods and countries, without an element of analysis. This implies, among other things, that comparisons over time only yield a very primitive forecasting which is based on a non-specified assumption of *ceteris paribus* and that comparisons of incomes pre-tax and incomes after complete redistribution cannot claim to show 'the influence of taxes' since the shifting phenomenon is disregarded. Hence the time needed to reduce inequality of gross incomes by one-half, as mentioned at the end of Section 2.4 – 50 to 85 years –, is in fact only a statement about the past. Similarly, the redistribution effects mentioned in Tables 2.II.A and B, culminating in the transfer of 13 per cent of national income in Denmark from the persons earning more to those earning less than the median income, also only warn us not to judge primary income inequality as if it were a true measure of income inequality. Perhaps a bit more can be claimed for the statements about the influence of *birth control* derived from Tables 2.V.A and B.

Chapter 3 goes one step further and essentially contains a number of partial models or *labour market models*, where only incomes and employment are endogenous and all 'explanatory' variables exogenous, including a number which are connected with incomes in the national economy. In most of the computations shown not incomes as such but their distribution, measured in one way or the other, are the variables 'to be explained' and correspondingly, the average levels and distribution measures of the supply and demand factors are the 'explanatory' variables. Supply is represented throughout this book by education *levels* and *distribution*. Demand is represented first (the simplest approach) by the *average income* of each observed unit (country, state, province or municipality) or (the next simple approach) by the *degree of industrialization* (or its counterpart, the agrarian level) or, finally, by a demand index which is a *weighted average* of the percentage of the labour force employed in agriculture, manufacturing, trade and commerce, and other services. The demand for qualified labour is lowest in agriculture and highest in 'other service' activities. The weights are the 'qualified-labour intensity' of the four main sectors.

The regression equations can be used to answer the question: Which changes in the explanatory variables reduce income inequality by one-half? Among the explanatory variables, education level and distribution are the ones concentrated on in most of this chapter. The answers show *considerable divergency*. For an inter-country comparison the answer is that 20 per cent more children in the age group 5–19 years should take part in education as compared with the 1960 level which already lay between 70% and 80% and 2 per cent more participation in the age group 20–29 (as compared to a participation level in 1960 of 2–7% in Europe and 12% in the USA). A time series inquiry for the Netherlands and Norway suggests that a doubling of the percentage of university-trained manpower would be needed. So does a cross-section study for the provinces of the Netherlands; but cross-section studies about American states and Canadian provinces give much less optimistic answers. Increases in education that are supposed to be realistic would only reduce, in some cases, the standard deviation of incomes by 10 per cent. The use of the demand index mentioned above yields better results again (Section 3.5). Much more optimistic answers are given also by other authors about the impact of average income growth (that is, economic development) on income inequality. This subject is taken up again in Chapter 6.

In a concluding section of Chapter 3 absolute incomes of groups of individuals with different years of schooling and years of working experience are compared; and it appears that group averages can be explained to a very high extent ($\overline{R} = 0.97$) by these two supply factors if a curvilinear relationship is assumed to exist. The completely different nature of this relation as compared with the ones discussed before is emphasized.

Chapter 4 tries to dig more deeply into the supply function by linking it up with *utility* or *welfare* functions and submits that welfare can be measured. As a very simple first approach welfare is supposed to depend, for averages of social groups, on income after taxes, schooling required for the job held and actual schooling. Schooling required is estimated on the basis of two alternative assumptions, one for about 20 occupational groups for the Netherlands, the other for seven American states. Numerical computations show that an additional parameter, called the degree of independence of decision-making, has to be added in order to explain income-after-tax differences. The income compensation desired for holding a job requiring higher schooling can be estimated in that manner and appears to be larger for Americans than for Dutchmen.

Chapter 5 tries to develop a theoretical basis for the demand for labour by the estimation of a *production function* in which five types of labour enter as production factors. It is a generalization of a Cobb–Douglas function, tested with the aid of material collected by Bowles and Dougherty for its substitution elasticity of unity between third-level educated and all other labour. Substitution elasticities between other types of labour are higher and of the orders of magnitude mentioned by these two authors.

After these preparations Chapter 6 reconsiders the influence of increased university education on the income distribution between university graduates and all other labour, taking into account the trend of technological development. The process is characterized as a *race between both developments* with education as the inequality depressing agent and technological development as the inequality boosting agent. During the period 1900–1990 both in the USA and in the Netherlands education appears as the victor and inequality has fallen considerably, so far, while there are prospects for some further fall. All this refers to primary incomes and hence in reality incomes have been more equalized.

Chapter 7 then presents a complete semi-macro model for the Netherlands in 1962, enabling us to tackle not only the problem of the *impact of more education* on income distribution, but also the problems of changes in *taxes* (including *shifting* possibilities) and in *technology*, if considered controllable (up to a point). One model is *analytical* and enables us to find the effect of given policy changes. The other is *normative* and yields the social optimum based on the assumption that social welfare is the weighted sum of groups' welfare, the weights being equal to the numbers of individuals in each group. Actual and optimal income distribution are shown for the Netherlands in Table 7.VI, for Illinois in Table 7.VII and for all seven USA states studied in Table 7.VIII.

Chapter 8 proposes a definition of *equitable income distribution*, namely a distribution of incomes and jobs such that all social groups show equal welfare. With the specification of the welfare function chosen in Chapter 4, equitable and optimal income distribution appear to be identical, but this is not true for all specifications.

Chapter 9 lists, first of all, the *institutions* and their instruments already used to influence income distribution, most of them aiming at less inequality. Subsequently it formulates some further proposals derived from the present study. These can be seen as proposed changes in social structure and will be summarized presently.

10.4. Changes in social structure

As announced in Section 1.1, no attempt has been made, in this study, to present in its entirety the social changes considered desirable by this author, or likely to occur in the coming decades. Only *changes closely connected* with income distribution changes have been considered. This implies a specification of those conceivable changes in social structure or order which are involved and, as a consequence, the recommendation of evolution rather than revolution, if the latter word stands for a sudden complete change. It is of some importance to stress that point, as will be discussed in Section 10.5. Social changes of particular significance for the attainment – *if at all possible* – of the optimum or of an equitable income distribution are:

(i) The extension of the *educational* system as a means of reducing the *gap* between the *demand* for and supply of the various types of labour used in the production process. Chapter 6 illustrates that substantial further reductions in inequality may result.

(ii) A *redirection of research* with respect to at least two points – research should aim at a technological development more in line with this equalization of demand for and supply of differing types of labour, and further research is needed on the concept of *equity* and the measurement of *welfare*. Research will have to be reoriented for several other reasons, such as the threatening world food and world energy situation; but, as explained, these subjects fall outside the scope of the present study.

(iii) A change of the *tax system* directed towards the attainment, through it, of optimal or equitable income distribution, or both. As we found in Chapter 7, the optimal tax system would be approached better if we were able to tax human *capabilities* themselves instead of their results, income. It remains to be seen, however, whether *psycho-technical tests* can be developed which are reliable enough to be used as a tax basis instead of income. This may be asking too much, but an attempt should be made. A discussion of the numerous misunderstandings about the type of tax meant and its impact had better be postponed until psycho-technical tests of sufficient reliability are available.

(iv) Higher taxes on *wealth, capital gains*, and *inherited estates* are a series of possibilities which have been under discussion for quite some time and which are only mentioned for the sake of completeness.

10.5. Implicit criticism of some alternative approaches

As a matter of course this study and the recommendations based on it imply *criticism* of a number of *alternative* approaches. This implicit criticism is addressed to three groups in particular. They will be briefly dealt with in succession.

(i) Traditional *interest groups*. Everywhere in society we come across opposition by vested interests which adhere to the maintenance of existing or historical income ratios. Thus, capital owners prefer to maintain their share in national income; highly paid employees or members of the free professions think the ratio of their income to that of lower paid employees or other citizens should be maintained. Entrepreneurs, whether big or small, claim something similar. All of them forget that the laws of demand and supply also apply to income, and not only to commodity markets, where they are so often seen as natural. *Group monopolies* of *well-paid* categories of labour cannot be ethically defended and run counter to the rules of liberal economics, not to speak of a more socially oriented set of rules as developed here.

(ii) *Marxists*, whether traditional or 'neo', attach more importance to the inequalities created by capital ownership in the old sense than to the inequalities created by human capital. They also tend to neglect the fact that the portion of national product allocated to capital owners has fallen considerably already and has fallen more for incomes after redistribution than for primary incomes. The suggestion that the *bourgeois élite* constitutes a *self-perpetuating group* needs the important correction that the number of people belonging to the élite of university graduates is expanding so that in the Netherlands in 1990 it will include ten times the percentage of the labour force it included in 1900. The élite is not only a group of a (more or less) self-perpetuating character, but is rapidly expanding. All this is not meant to imply that Marx has not contributed to our understanding of society or that Marxists don't put their finger on socially unhealthy situations every once in a while. If they do so with the aid of proper scientific methods, their contribution can be constructive.

(iii) For completeness' sake I mention *anarchist* groups; I don't formulate any more precise objection to their theory than the very general one that I think that society needs a government and that complete freedom for any group is incompatible with the other groups' complete freedom.

10.6. Further research needed

It is hardly necessary to stress again that further research is needed. Science is always in need of it – science is never finished. For our subject this is clear enough, every chapter of this book leaves a number of unanswered questions.

This is true, first of all, for the *information* available. We are in urgent need of more information on human *capabilities* relevant to the production process in the widest sense. We are in need also of better income data and of more administrative checks on *tax evasion* as part of such better data. Some forms of increasing tax evasion these days will be very difficult to identify. The need for further research on *production functions* with many types of labour, as initiated by Bowles, Dougherty and Psacharopoulos, is evident too. Particular stress may be laid on the need for an intensive discussion on and elaboration of what has been proposed about the measurement of utility. Here Van Praag and his collaborators should again be mentioned as pioneers. A further elaboration of the concept of *optimal social order*, now undertaken by Waardenburg, is of equal importance. The reader will no doubt be able to add a long list of further research proposals.

References

[1] A. B. Atkinson, Poverty in Britain and the reform of social security, Cambridge, 1969.
[2] R. Bentzel, Inkomstfördelningen i Sverige, Uppsala, 1953 (Income distribution in Sweden (diss.); Swedish).
[3] Kj. Bjerke, Changes in the Danish income distribution 1939-1952, Income and Wealth Series VI, London, 1956, p. 98.
[4] G. K. Boon, Economic choice of human and physical factors in production, Amsterdam, 1964.
[5] S. Bowles, Planning educational systems for economic growth, Cambridge, Mass., 1969.
[6] S. Bowles and H. Gintis, IQ in the U.S. class structure, Social Policy 3, 1972/3, p. 1. Cf. also S. Bowles, The genetic inheritance of IQ and the intergenerational reproduction of economic inequality, Harvard Institute of Economic Research Discussion Paper no. 253, Cambridge, Mass., September 1972.
[7] E. C. Budd, Postwar changes in the size distribution of incomes in the United States, American Economic Review, Papers and Proceedings, May 1970, p. 247.
[8] Bureau van Statistiek, Amsterdam, Huishoudrekeningen van 212 gezinnen uit verschillende kringen der bevolking - 1923/4, Amsterdam, 1927 (Family budgets of 212 families from different population strata in Amsterdam - 1923/4; Dutch).
[9] L. S. Burns and H. E. Frech III, Human capital and the size distribution of income in Dutch cities, De Economist 118, 1970, p. 598.
[10] Central Bureau of Statistics of the Netherlands, Huishoudrekeningen van 598 gezinnen - 1935/36, The Hague, 1938 (Budgets of 598 families in the Netherlands - 1935/36; Dutch).
[11] Central Bureau of Statistics of the Netherlands, Recente ontwikkelingen in de inkomensverdeling van Nederland en enkele andere landen, Statistische en Econometrische Onderzoekingen, 1960, p. 51 (Recent changes in the income distribution in the Netherlands and selected other countries; Dutch with English summary).
[12] Central Bureau of Statistics of the Netherlands, 13e Algemene Volkstelling - 31 mei 1960, Deel 14, The Hague, 1966, p. 85 (13th Census of 31 May 1960, Part 14; Dutch); and: Inkomensverdeling 1960, Regionale gegevens, Zeist, 1964, p. 118 (Income Distribution 1960, Regional Data; Dutch).

[13] Central Bureau of Statistics of the Netherlands, Zeventig jaren statistiek in tijdreeksen, The Hague, 1970 (Seventy years of statistics in
time series; Dutch).

[14] B. R. Chiswick, The average level of schooling and the intraregional
inequality of income: A clarification, American Economic Review
LVIII, 1968, p. 495.

[15] B. R. Chiswick, Earnings inequality and economic development,
Quarterly Journal of Economics LXXXV, 1971, p. 21.

[16] B. R. Chiswick, Income inequality; Regional analyses within a human
capital framework, New York, 1974.

[17] D. Cole and J. E. G. Utting, The distribution of household and individual income, Income and Wealth Series VI, London, 1956, p. 239.

[18] V. M. Dandekar and M. Rath, Poverty in India, Economic and
Political Weekly VI, 1971, p. 25 (2 Jan.), p. 106 (9 Jan.).

[19] H. Deleek, Maatschappelijke zekerheid en inkomensverdeling in
België, Louvain, 1966 (Social security and income distribution in
Belgium; Dutch).

[20] P. de Wolff and A. R. D. van Slijpe, The relation between income,
intelligence, education and social background, Institute of Actuarial
Science and Econometrics, University of Amsterdam, 1972.

[21] C. R. S. Dougherty, Substitution and the structure of the labour
force, The Economic Journal 82, 1972, p. 170.

[22] C. R. S. Dougherty, Estimates of labour aggregation functions,
Harvard Center for International Affairs, Economic Development
Report no. 190 (Development Research Group), Cambridge, Mass.,
March 1971.

[23] O. D. Duncan, Path analysis: Sociological examples, American
Journal of Sociology 72, 1966, p. 1.

[24] R. B. Freeman, The market for college-trained manpower, Cambridge,
Mass., 1971.

[25] R. Frisch, Pitfalls in the statistical construction of demand and supply
curves, Veröffentlichungen der Frankfurter Gesellschaft für Kon-
junkturforschung (herausgegeben von E. Altschul), Neue Folge 5,
Leipzig, 1933.

[26] R. Frisch, Confluence analysis, Oslo, 1934.

[27] S. A. Goldberg and R. Podoluk, Income size distribution statistics
in Canada – A survey and some analysis, Income and Wealth Series
VI, London, 1956, p. 155.

[28] S. F. Goldsmith, Impact of the income tax on socio-economic groups
of families in the United States, Income and Wealth Series X, London,
1964, p. 248.

[29] Hamburg in Zahlen, 1965, p. 290; 1966, p. 149 (Hamburg in figures;
German).

[30] F. L. Hitchcock, The distribution of a product from several sources
to numerous localities, Journal of Mathematical Physics 20, 1941,
p. 224.

[31] T. Husén, Ability, opportunity and career; A 26 year follow-up,
Education Research 10, 1968, p. 170.

[32] H. J. Jaksch, Income distribution as an objective in development planning, De Economist 122, 1974, p. 1.

[33] C. Jencks, Inequality: A reassessment of the effect of family and schooling in America, New York, 1972.

[34] A. R. Jensen, Genetics and education, London, 1972.

[35] N. Kaldor, The reform of personal taxation, in: Essays on economic policy, vol. 1, London, 1964, p. 203.

[36] P. G. Keat, Long-run changes in occupational wage structure 1900–1956, Journal of Political Economy 68, 1960, p. 584.

[37] S. K. Kuipers, Inkomensnivellering, Preadvies voor de Vereniging voor de Staathuishoudkunde, The Hague, 1973 (Income equalization, Report to the Economic Association of the Netherlands; Dutch).

[38] S. Kuznets, Modern economic growth, New Haven, 1966.

[39] Labor, 18th Report of the Commissioner for Labor – 1903, Cost of living and retail prices of food, Part I, Washington, 1904, pp. 582–583.

[40] R. J. Lampman, Transfer approaches to distribution policy, American Economic Review, Papers and Proceedings, May 1970, p. 270.

[41] H. F. Lydall, The long-term trend in the size distribution of income, Journal of the Royal Statistical Society A 122, 1959, p. 1.

[42] H. F. Lydall, The structure of earnings, Oxford, 1968.

[43] L. B. M. Mennes, J. Tinbergen and J. G. Waardenburg, The element of space in development planning, Amsterdam–London, 1969, pp. 38 ff.

[44] J. Mincer, The distribution of labor incomes: A survey with special reference to the human capital approach, The Journal of Economic Literature VIII, 1970, p. 1.

[45] J. Mincer, Schooling, experience and earnings, N.B.E.R., New York, 1974.

[46] J. L. Nicholson, Redistribution of income in the United Kingdom in 1959, 1957 and 1953, Income and Wealth Series X, London, 1964, p. 148.

[47] Norge (Norway): Historisk statistikk 1968, Oslo, 1969 (Historical statistics; Norwegian).

[48] Nota over de inkomensverdeling, Bijlage 15 Miljoenennota 1970, The Hague, 1969 (Memorandum on the income distribution, Annex 15, to the State budget 1970, Parliamentary Document Session 1969–1970, no. 10 300; Dutch).

[49] O.E.C.D., Statistics of the occupation and education structure of the labour force in 53 countries, Paris, 1969, p. 114.

[50] J. Passenier, Een arbeidsmarkt vol academici, Intermediair, 27 October 1972, p. 1 (A labour market filled with university graduates; Dutch).

[51] Ch. Perelman, De la justice, Brussels, 1945 (On justice; French).

[52] G. Psacharopoulos and K. Hinchliffe, Further evidence on the elasticity of substitution among different types of educated labor, Journal of Political Economy 80, 1972, p. 786.

[53] L. A. J. Quetelet, De l'homme, Brussels, 1835 (On man; French).

[54] Råd, Det økonomiske, Formandskabet, Den personlige indkomst-

fordeling of indkomstjævningen over de offentlige finanser, Copenhagen, 1967 (Presidency of the Economic Council: The personal income distribution and income redistribution through public finance; Danish).

[55] J. Rawls, A theory of justice, Cambridge, Mass., 1971.

[56] Reichsamt, Statistisches, Die Lebenshaltung von 2000 Arbeiter-, Angestellten- und Beamtenhaushaltungen 1927/28, Teil I, Berlin, 1932, p. 14 (The level of living of 2000 worker, employee and civil servant families 1927/28; German).

[57] P. J. Roscam Abbing, Ethiek van de inkomensverdeling, Deventer, 1973 (Ethics of income distribution; Dutch).

[58] T. P. Schultz, The distribution of personal income: Case study of the Netherlands, unpublished dissertation, M.I.T., Cambridge, Mass., 1965.

[59] T. W. Schultz, The economic value of education, New York, 1963.

[60] L. Soltow, Toward income equality in Norway, Madison, 1965, p. 55.

[61] Statistical abstract of the United States, 1972, p. 111.

[62] J. Tinbergen, The theory of the optimum regime, in: Selected papers, Amsterdam, 1959, p. 264.

[63] J. Tinbergen, A positive and a normative theory of income distribution, Review of Income and Wealth 16, 1970, p. 221.

[64] J. Tinbergen, Can income inequality be reduced further?, Festschrift für Walter Georg Waffenschmidt, Meisenheim am Glan, 1971.

[65] J. Tinbergen, An interdisciplinary approach to the measurement of utility, The Economic and Social Research Institute Fifth Geary Lecture, Dublin, 1972.

[66] J. Tinbergen, The impact of education on income distribution, Review of Income and Wealth 18, 1972, p. 255.

[67] J. Tinbergen, Labour with different types of skills and jobs as production factors, De Economist 121, 1973, p. 213.

[68] J. Tinbergen, Actual vs optimal income distribution in a three-level education model, Scritti in onore di Gugliemo Tagliacarne, Roma, 1974, p. 539.

[69] J. Tinbergen, Substitution between types of labour in production, to be published in a volume in honour of Professor Del Vecchio.

[70] J. Tinbergen, De wedloop tussen technische ontwikkeling en opleiding, forthcoming in Liber Amicorum Prof. Dr. Gaston Eyskens (The race between technological development and education; Dutch).

[71] J. Tinbergen, Consequences of the existence of 'immobile industries', International economics and development in honour of Raúl Prebisch, New York, 1972.

[72] J. Tinbergen, A true question of coexistence, Coexistence 11, 1974.

[73] R. H. Tuck, An essay on the economic theory of rank, Oxford, 1953.

[74] C. J. Ullman, The growth of professional occupations in the American labor force: 1900–1963, World Bank paper based on Columbia University dissertation, 1972.

[75] United Nations, Economic survey of Europe in 1956, Geneva, 1957, ch. IX, p. 6.

[76] United Nations, Economic survey of Europe in 1956, Geneva, 1957, ch. IX, p. 22.

[77] United Nations Research Institute for Social Development (UNRISD), Compilation of development indicators (for 1960), Geneva, 1969.

[78] United States Census of Population, Occupation by earnings and education, Washington, p. 2.

[79] B. M. S. van Praag, The welfare function of income in Belgium : An empirical investigation, European Economic Review 2, 1971, p. 337.

[80] B. M. S. van Praag and A. Kapteyn, Further evidence on the individual welfare function of income : An empirical investigation in the Netherlands, European Economic Review 4, 1973, p. 33.

[81] V. Volterra, Leçons sur la théorie mathématique de la lutte pour la vie, Paris, 1931 (Lessons on the mathematical theory of the struggle for life; French).

[82] H. Vos, Enige kwantitatieve onderzoekingen over de betrekkingen tussen overheidsfinanciën en volkshuishouding, Haarlem, 1946, p. 53 (Some quantitative investigations on the relations between public finance and the economy; Dutch).

[83] P. J. D. Wiles and S. Markowski, Income distribution under communism and capitalism, Soviet Studies, 1970/1, p. 344, p. 487.

[84] Wirtschaft und Statistik, Einkommensverhältnisse der Haushalte (Ergebnis der 1%-Wohnungsstichprobe 1965), Wirtschaft und Statistik, 1969, p. 366 (Income relations of households; Results of 1 per cent dwelling sample 1965; German).

Subject Index

Author Index